Identities

Other Books by Irving Weiss

Visual Poetry

Visual Voices: The Poem As a Print Object
Number Poems
Infrapics: Xerolage 35

Translations from Malcolm de Chazal

Plastic Sense
Sens-Plastique
Sens-Plastique (Complete edition)

Reference Books with Anne D. Weiss

American Authors and Books: 1640 to the Present Day
Thesaurus of Book Digests: 1950-1980
Reflections on Childhood

Identities

by Irving Weiss

2012
Xexoxial Editions
West Lima, Wisconsin

Some of these poems were previously published in:

A Journal of the Arts, Anthology Spidertangle, Black Box, Caliban, Cauldron, Difference Engine, Drunken Boat , Lost and Found Times, Koja, Manglar, The Montserrat Review, Muse Apprentice Guild, Otoliths, Project Hope, Ubu Web, Wordseen Group Exhibit, Rampike, Rio: International Review, Synaesthetic, Score, Signal, Stream, Transmog, Van, Visible Language, Word for/Word, and in other versions in my previous collections Infrapics, Number Poems, and Visual Voices: The Poem As a Print Object.

Online at:
http://xexoxial.org/is/identities/by/irving_weiss

ISBN-10: 1-936687-04-6
ISBN-13: 978-1-936687-04-6

published by
Xexoxial Editions
10375 County Hway Alphabet
La Farge, WI 54639

www.xexoxial.org
perspicacity@xexoxial.org

For Bruna, without whom. . . .

We have divided matter into three parts, evaluating them according to their different capacities for remaining erect: solid on its legs, liquid sitting down, and gas collapsed everywhere. All forms of life on earth would feel hard to the ethereal plasticity of an angel's touch. Seen from an unearthly distance above, the three arbitrary classifications of solid, liquid, and gas would appear like one undifferentiated block of matter. Animals simply do not have our idea of solid, liquid, and gas: their senses lead them to "other" conclusions. People from Mars, Jupiter, and the Earth and the Moon must have altogether different physical conceptions of matter. Each one biologically assimilates his world in his own way. Our ambience is more or less tough to the bite of our senses according to the length of their teeth.

–Malcolm de Chazal, Sens-Plastique

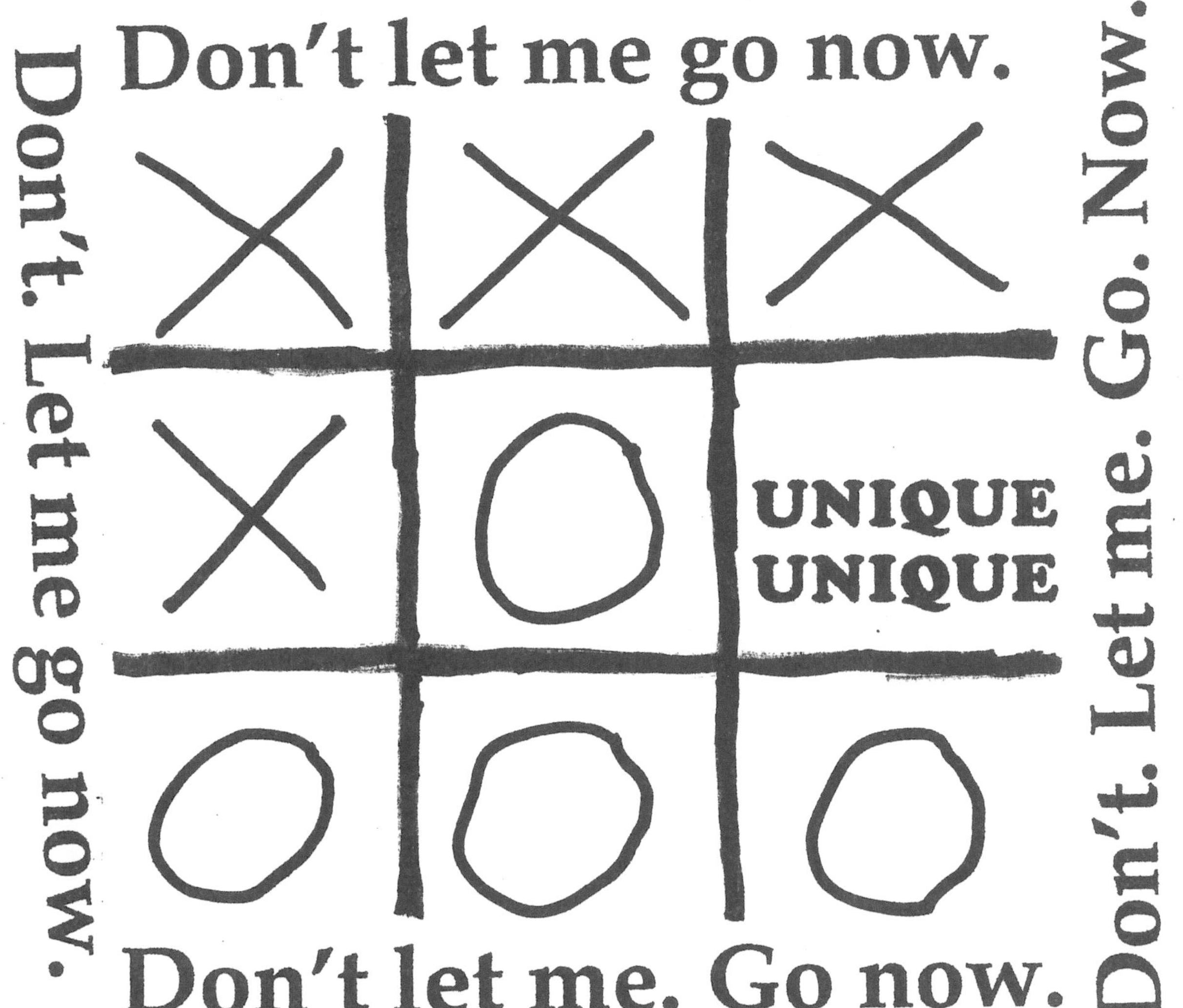
Don't let me go now.
Don't. Let me go now.
UNIQUE
UNIQUE
Don't. Let me. Go. Now.
Don't let me. Go now.

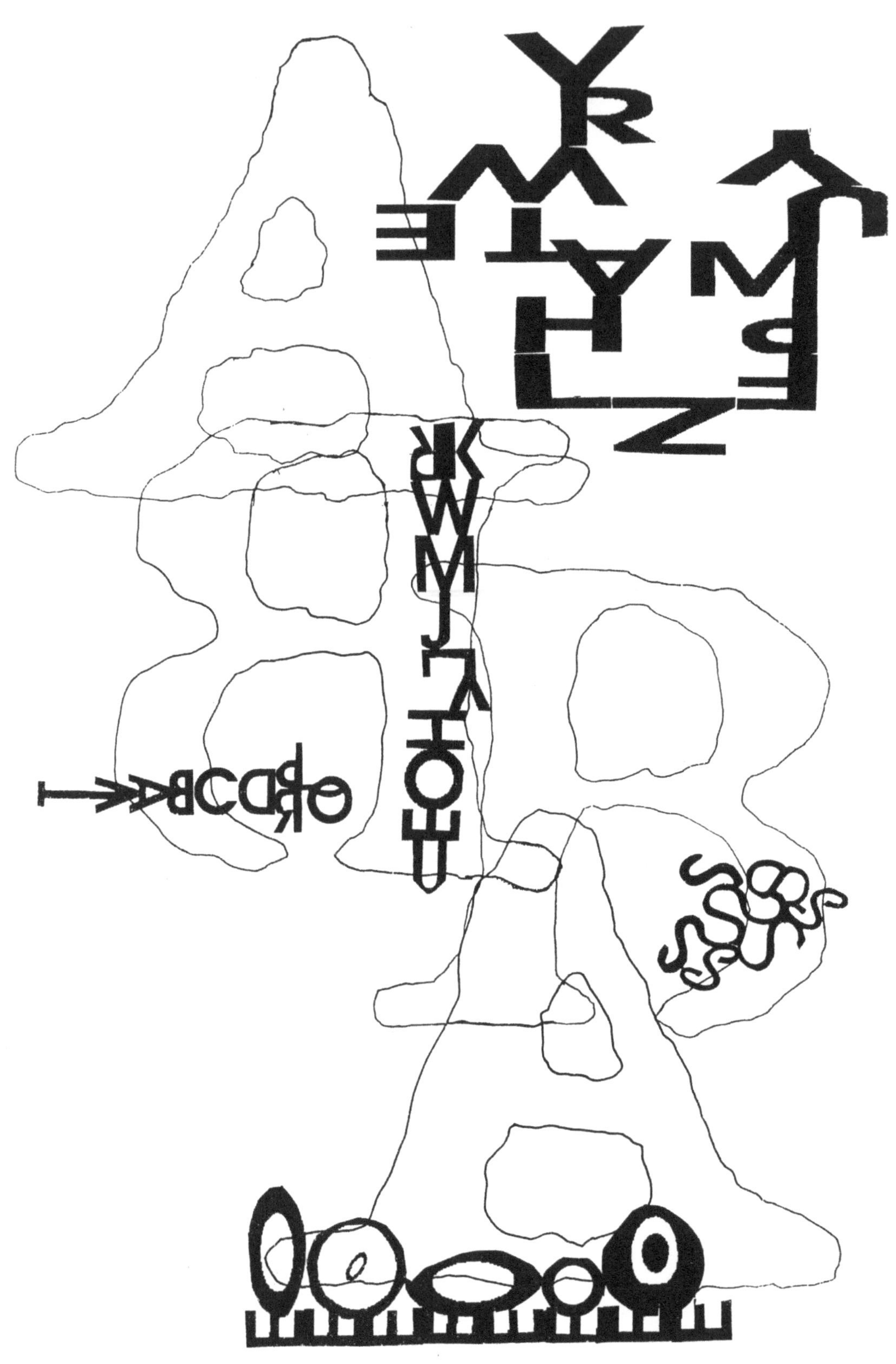

Blotch (blɒtʃ). [A comparatively recent word, with no cognates outside Eng. App. an onomatopœic modification of BLOT, for which it is commonly used dialectally: the sound seems to express a broader spreading *blot*, of the nature of a *patch*. But in sense 1 there may have been association with the earlier BOTCH. The suggestion that it is a variant of BLATCH 'blacking', finds no support in the history of either word.]

1. An inflamed eruption, or discoloured patch, on the skin; a pustule, boil, or botch.

1604 [see BLOTCHED]. 1669 W. SIMPSON *Hydrol. Chym.* 72 In its road it leaves its character of Spots, ...ins, Blotches, Buboes, Ulcers, &c. in..the skin. 1711 ... No. 16 P 2 Healing those Blotches and Tumours ... in the Body. 1740 CHEYNE *Regimen* Pref. ... of Infancy are generally Scabs, Blotch... the Face, etc. 1866 ROGERS *Agric. & Prices* ... blotches appear on the skin.

fig. 1882 FARRAR *Early Chr.* II. ... they regarded Gentiles as worthless, ... as little better than a blotch on the healt...

b. *spec.* A disease in dogs.

1824 *Annals Sporting* VI. 265, I found ... hibited appearances of a disease .. termed ...

2. A large irregular spot or blot ... co... etc.; a dab or patch.

1768 TUCKER *Lt. Nat.* II. 306 To brush off the soil .. and not suffer it to gather in pitchy blotches upon the surface. 1807 SIR R. WILSON in *Life* II. vii. 83 The snow fell in large blotches. 1870 H. MACMILLAN *Bible Teach.* x. 201 Its leaves are covered with brown unsightly blotches. 1873 MOGGRIDGE *Ants & Spiders* II. 76 Four blotches of paler colour.

b. *fig.* = BLOT 2.

1860 HAWTHORNE *Marble Faun* (1879) II. xii. 122 Ignoring all moral blotches...

c. *transf.* ... clumsy daub.

1860 SMILES ... iv. 71 The artist .. attempting to produce a brilli... ...ect at a dash, will only produce a blotch.

d. A shapeless object.

1872 BROWNING *Fifine* lxxix. 17 Catch the puniest .. And, as you nip the blotch 'twixt thumb and fingernail, etc.

3. = BLOT (of ink). (North of Eng. and Scotl.)

18... ...KINSON *Provinc. Danby*, *Blotch*, a blot, in a copy-b... a clean piece of paper. *Blotch paper*, blotting ... BLOTCHING, BLOTCHY.]

... (blɒtʃ), *v.* [f. prec. sb.]

... To mark or cover with blotches.

1604 [see BLOTCHED]. 1774 GOLDSM. *Hist. Earth* v. 79 The tail is..irregularly barred and blotched with an obscure ash colour. 1853 KANE *Grinnell Exp.* xxxii. (1856) 281 A great pla... ...otched by dark, jagged shadows. 1865 BARING-... *Werewolves* vi. 75 Its walls were blotched with lichen.

... = BLOT *v.*[1] (Common in Scotl. and north of Eng., as 'He has blotched two pages of his book.') Cf. BLOTCHING, BLOTCHY.

Blotched (blɒtʃt), *ppl. a.* [f. prec. vb. + -ED.] Marked, discoloured, or covered with blotches.

1604 DRAYTON *Moses* II. 328 To giue their bloch'd and blister'd bodies ease. 1785 BURNS *Ep. J. M'Math* xii, ... blotch't and foul wi' mony a stain. 1870 HOOKER ... *Flora* 252 *Pulmonaria officinalis*, Leaves .. always ...ched with pale green.

Blotching, *vbl. sb.* [f. as prec. + -ING[1].] The action of marking with blotches, discolouring.

1767 *Specif. T. Long's Patent* No. 869 A machine for the b... 1872 DANA ... ...s shades ...

BOTCHED BLOT!

... CARLYLE ... IX. ... i. 6 Read him with a ... yourself what the real names are, out of ... blotching made of them.

...*ppl.* ... That makes blotches.

1865 RUSKIN *Sesame* 32 Owing to the spread of a shallow, blotching, blundering, infectious 'information' everywhere, and to the teaching of catechisms and phrases at schools.

Blotchy (blɒtʃi), *a.* [f. BLOTCH *sb.* + -Y[1].] Characterized by blotches or blotching.

1824–9 LANDOR *Wks.* (1853) II. 107 Slim, straddling, blotchy writers. 1860 *All Y. Round* 545 The vaults themselves have..got blotchy and bepimpled.

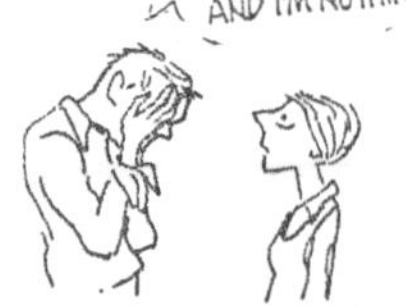
I CAN'T TALK TO THAT LITTLE RED-HAIRED GIRL BECAUSE SHE'S SOMETHING AND I'M NOTHING

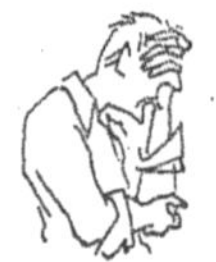
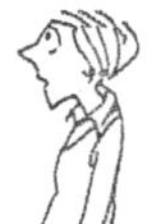
IF I WERE SOMETHING AND SHE WERE NOTHING, I COULD TALK TO HER, OR IF SHE WERE SOMETHING AND I WERE SOMETHING, THEN I COULD TALK TO HER...

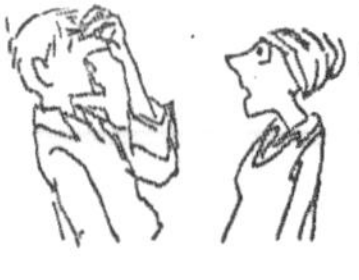
OR IF SHE WERE NOTHING AND I WERE NOTHING, THEN I ALSO COULD TALK TO HER...BUT SHE'S SOMETHING AND I'M NOTHING SO I CAN'T TALK TO HER...

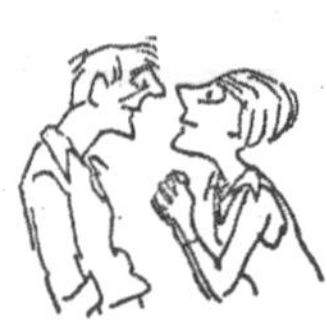
FOR A NOTHING, CHARLIE BROWN, YOU'RE REALLY SOMETHING!

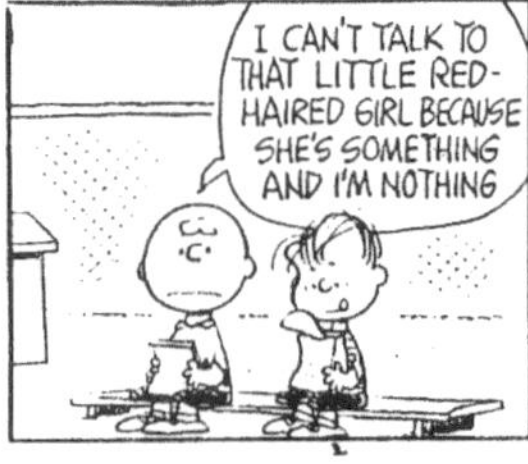
I CAN'T TALK TO THAT LITTLE RED-HAIRED GIRL BECAUSE SHE'S SOMETHING AND I'M NOTHING

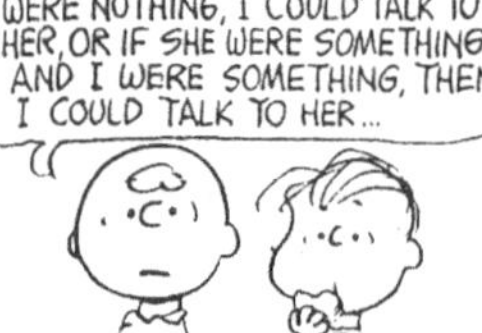
IF I WERE SOMETHING AND SHE WERE NOTHING, I COULD TALK TO HER, OR IF SHE WERE SOMETHING AND I WERE SOMETHING, THEN I COULD TALK TO HER...

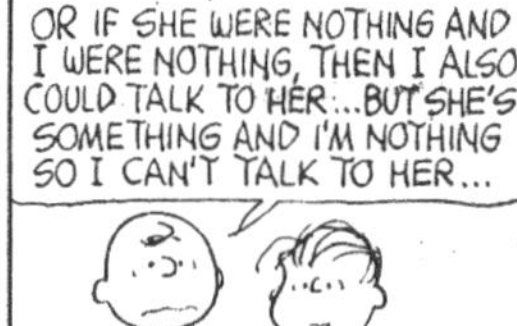
OR IF SHE WERE NOTHING AND I WERE NOTHING, THEN I ALSO COULD TALK TO HER...BUT SHE'S SOMETHING AND I'M NOTHING SO I CAN'T TALK TO HER...

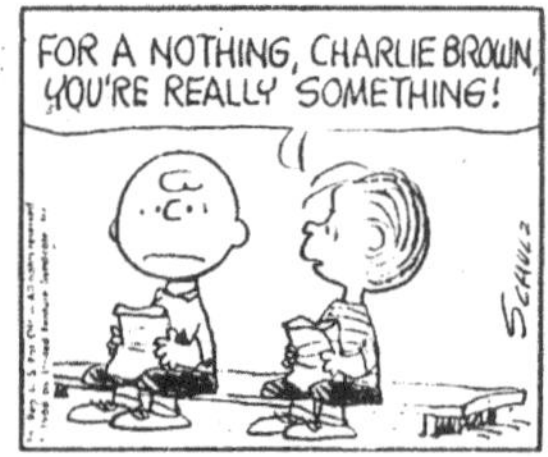
FOR A NOTHING, CHARLIE BROWN, YOU'RE REALLY SOMETHING!
SCHULZ

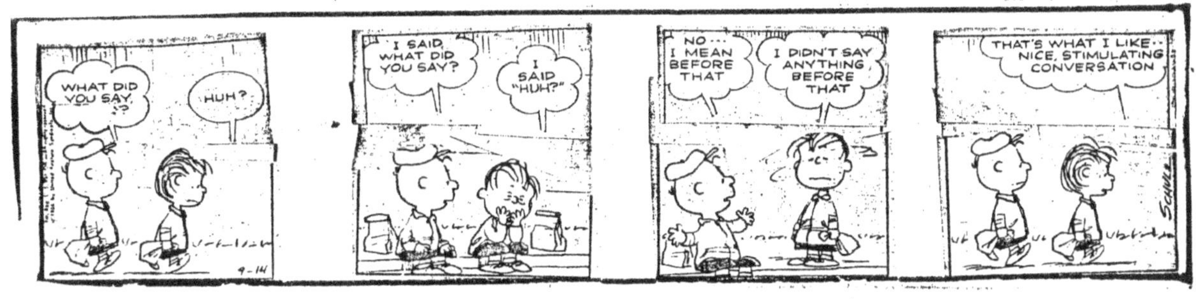
WHAT DID YOU SAY ?
HUH?
I SAID, WHAT DID YOU SAY?
I SAID "HUH?"
NO... I MEAN BEFORE THAT
I DIDN'T SAY ANYTHING BEFORE THAT
THAT'S WHAT I LIKE.. NICE, STIMULATING CONVERSATION

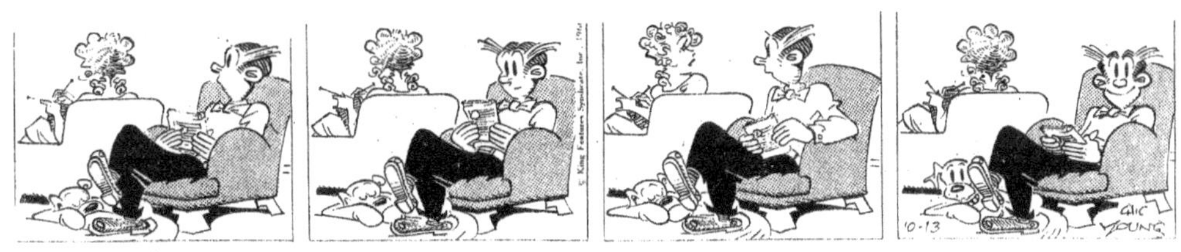

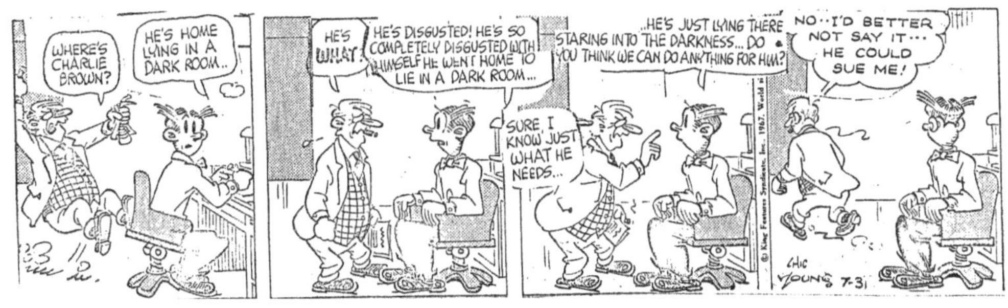
WHERE'S CHARLIE BROWN?
HE'S HOME LYING IN A DARK ROOM..
HE'S WHAT?
HE'S DISGUSTED! HE'S SO COMPLETELY DISGUSTED WITH HIMSELF HE WENT HOME TO LIE IN A DARK ROOM...
..HE'S JUST LYING THERE STARING INTO THE DARKNESS... DO YOU THINK WE CAN DO ANYTHING FOR HIM?
SURE, I KNOW JUST WHAT HE NEEDS...
NO.. I'D BETTER NOT SAY IT... HE COULD SUE ME!

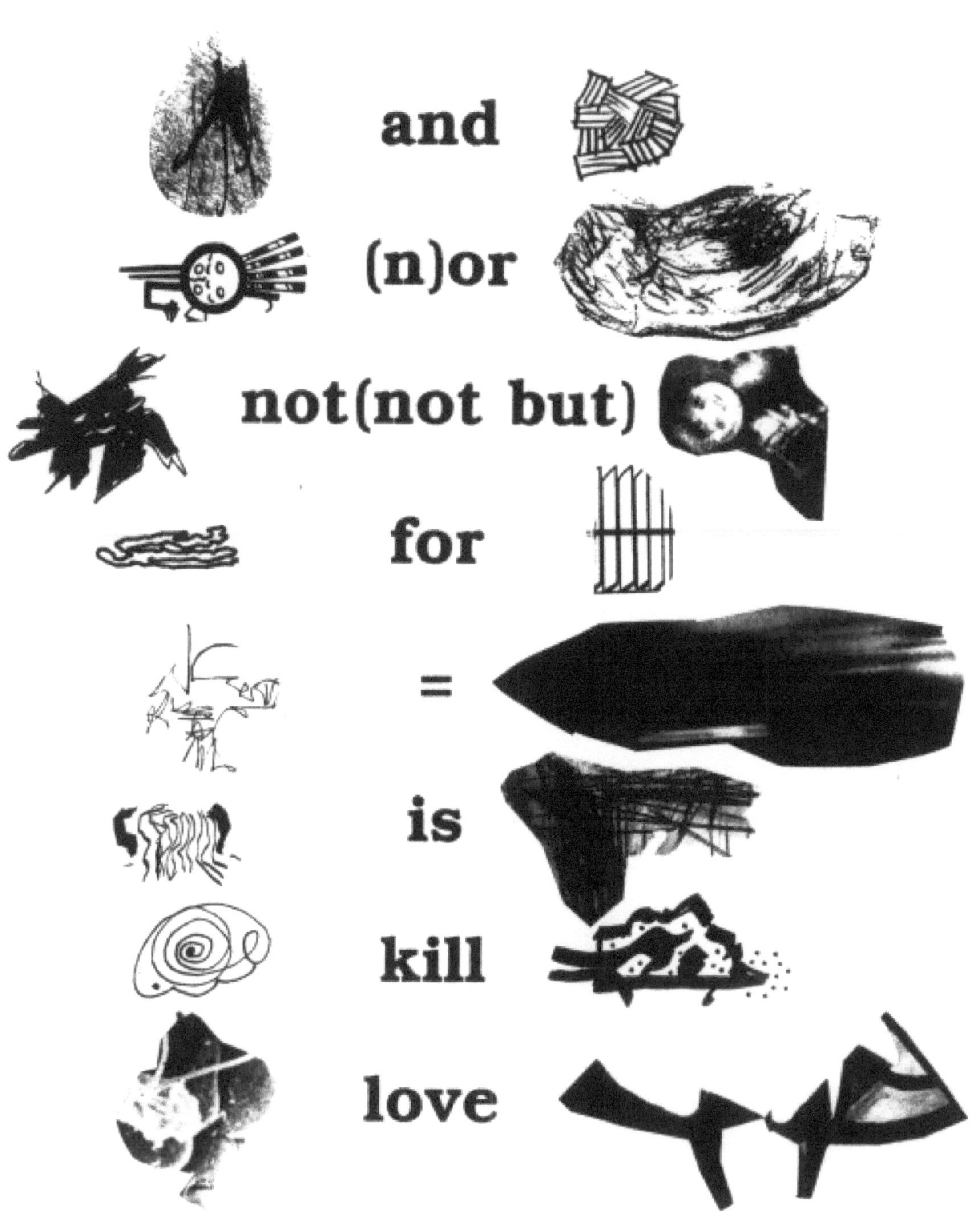
and
(n)or
not(not but)
for
=
is
kill
love

An All-Long-Poems-Meet-in-the-Middle Poem

Milton, *Paradise Regained,* Book 3, ll. 47-118

Butler, *Hudibras,* Part III, Canto iiii, ll. 795-859 & 915-920

Blake, *Vala, or The Four Zoas,* "Night the Eighth"

LIGHT

BIRTH **STEALTH** **HEARTH**

MIGHT

BREATH **BREATH** **BREATH**

FIGHT

CENSORED

OOLBLOOBDBODOLBLOODOBDOLLOBODOBOD

PLIGHT

EARTH **TILTH** **WORTH**

FLIGHT

STEALTH **HEATH** **DEATH**

NIGHT

The Cliffs of Eddies Wrath

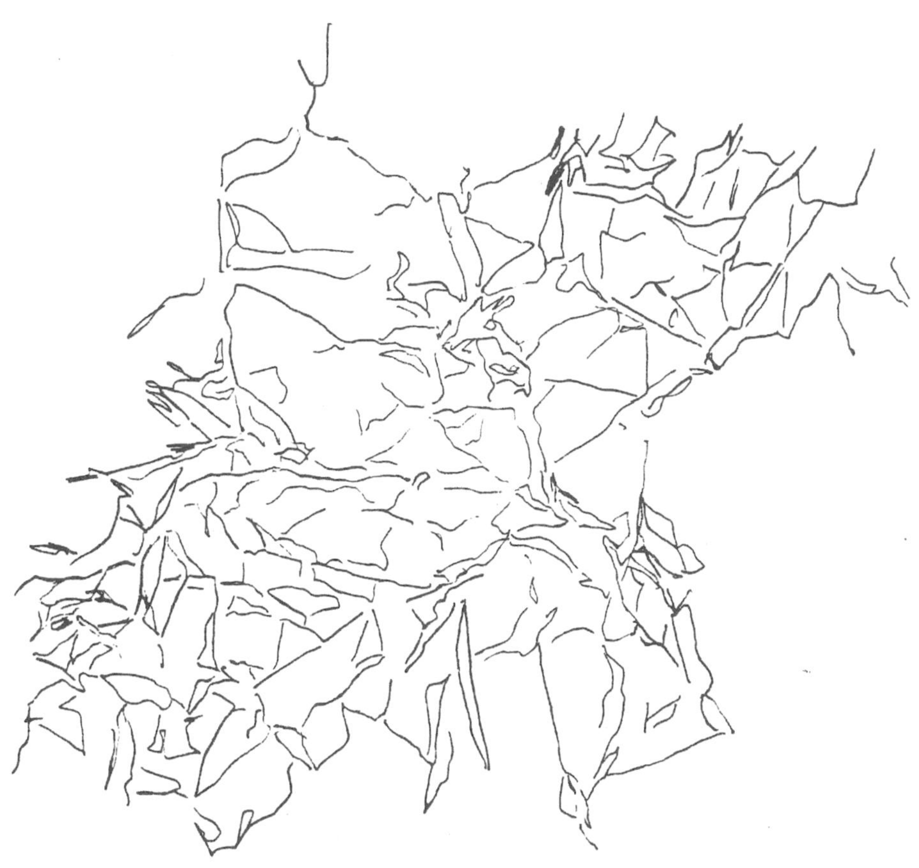

you dont write across the sky
said 7 year old edward burne jones
when mr caswell made his comments
on eddies drawing of a deer in a field
directly on eddies drawing

i have crumpled this sheet of paper
into a tight ball
and then unfolding it flat
traced the veins of wrinkling
as the cliffs of eddies wrath
where the massif of outrage clumps together

and say so here
in the southeastern corner of the zenith
where nothing else is happening

Brooding Grunt Chant Scheme

aggh**r** thing! thag!

Agghr ogres thing! thag!

A. Rouged thugs thing thag

A. Grudged orgies raging thing thag

A. Goths glut cringe gnarl thing thag

A. Gnashing thicket gnouts clang oaths thing thag

A. Muck screeching fang clog gut gouged crag thing thag!

A. Sludges bludgeon chigger dredge flog slung edgy thing thag!

A. Dangling crotch knuckle juggled conk flung chinch dudgeon thing

t

h

a g !

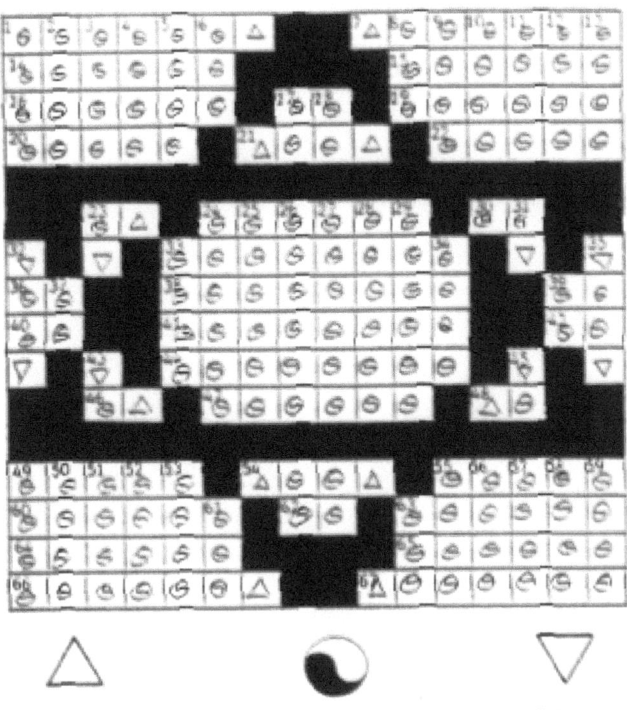

ACROSS

1. Thing
7. Dart
14. Little finger
15. Root
16. Pistol
17. Penis
19. Wang
20. Yard
21. Horn
22. Roger
23. Three inches
24. Dong
30. Weapon
33. Dick
36. Hot dog
38. Bugle
39. Cock
40. Lingam
41. Schlong
42. Hook
44. Pole
46. Snake
47. Steed
48. Soldier
49. Banger
54. Schmuck
55. Sword
60. P****k
62. Schwanz
63. Nose
64. Diver
65. Tickler
66. John Thomas
67. It

DOWN

1. Thing
2. Nest
3. Flower
4. Slit
5. Plum
6. Ling
8. Home
9. Vagina
10. Place
11. Darkness
12. Snatch
13. Muff
17. Beaver
18. Twat
23. Treasure
24. Hole
25. Yoni
26. Lap
27. Et cetera
28. Coun
29. Den
31. Netherlands
32. Glove
33. Circle
34. C**t
35. Eye
37. Box
39. Pussy
43. Wound
45. Africa
49. Slash
50. Tail
51. Pool
52. City
53. Fort
55. Maidenhead
56. Commodity
57. Ultimate goal
58. Jerusalem
59. Ass
61. Belly
63. It

permposition, two there also. Blue and bluish colors of patches, smears, blurs, mostly curved in the southwest-northeast diagonal. White streaks, faint, mostly upright. Background grey-oyster-white. Basic color layer in patches and smears (as described above) over the background. Forces of relation or contention: ruled rectangles; dark-heavy linear-packed curved smears, patches, scribble-concentrations, blue and blackish: and numbers. I am ~~reading~~ reading ~~all~~ all the above and below remarks into what I see as the result of taking the ~~time~~ time to look, and as I can respect or not the integrity of the painting I can write my statement into it as I do here partially, but no more than here because I don't want to cancel it out my writing about it. It must scoffing out of anxiety. It asks for looking. Out of it quadrilateral integrity and presume importance. But is it worth being analyzed because it demands to be looked at so closely that putting analysis into words becomes a critical duty or because one wonders what it is at all and therefore must

Drifting movement from lower left diagonally through to upper right, carrying numbers, slashes of color, black and violet scribbles, triangles and rectangles of different hardness and softness of design and inscription across. A blotchy snake-nosed blunt scribbled protrusion from upper right side. Numbers: 80 in dark red, 240, 1267 in sequence, 21, 3, 2 4280, 267, 81, 4, but others as well, and among them those that are only faintly distinguishable as well as scribble-lines that are only hardly ~~sound~~ numbers.

...a very greenish grey rather. And the whole expanse of the pictorial scene shimmers and "moves" because of the different tones, scribble depths, and diagonal sweep. The center of attention is a cross of a "y"

Untitled, 1969 (Bolsena) oil, chalk...

GLOSS TWOMBLY

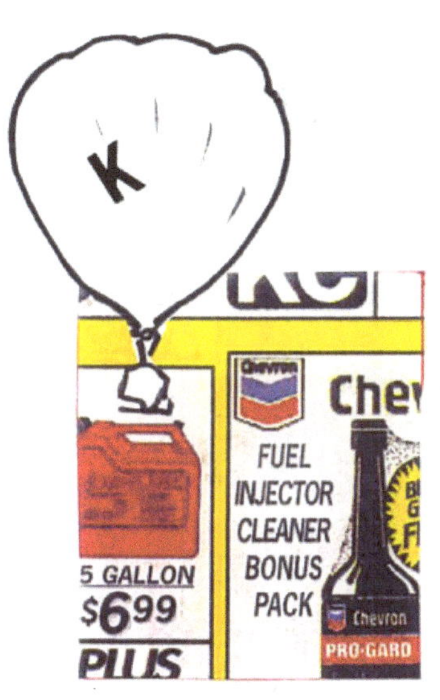

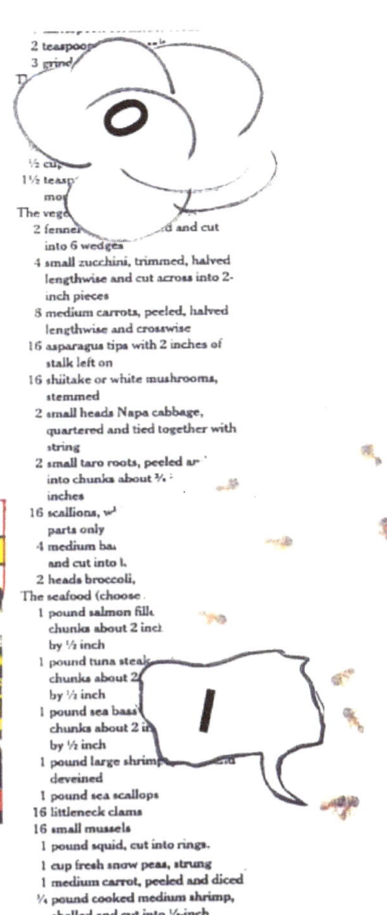

2 teaspoo
3 grind
½ cu
1½ teasp
mo
The vege
2 fenne d and cut into 6 wedges
4 small zucchini, trimmed, halved lengthwise and cut across into 2-inch pieces
8 medium carrots, peeled, halved lengthwise and crosswise
16 asparagus tips with 2 inches of stalk left on
16 shiitake or white mushrooms, stemmed
2 small heads Napa cabbage, quartered and tied together with string
2 small taro roots, peeled a into chunks about ¾ inches
16 scallions, w parts only
4 medium ba and cut into
2 heads broccoli,
The seafood (choose
1 pound salmon fill chunks about 2 inc by ½ inch
1 pound tuna steak chunks about 2 by ½ inch
1 pound sea bass chunks about 2 i by ½ inch
1 pound large shrimp deveined
1 pound sea scallops
16 littleneck clams
16 small mussels
1 pound squid, cut into rings.
1 cup fresh snow peas, strung
1 medium carrot, peeled and diced
¾ pound cooked medium shrimp, shelled and cut into ¼-inch pieces
6 ounces lump crab meat, picked over to remove cartilage
1 cup cooked sticky (glutinous) rice
1 medium-size jalapeño pepper, stemmed and minced (with seeds)
1 medium-size clove garlic, peeled and minced
1½ teaspoons minced fresh ginger
2 teaspoons grated lemon zest
2 teaspoons fresh lemon juice
1½ teaspoons kosher salt
1 package 6½-inch round rice paper
The sauce and garnish:
¼ cup sugar
½ cup nuoc mam

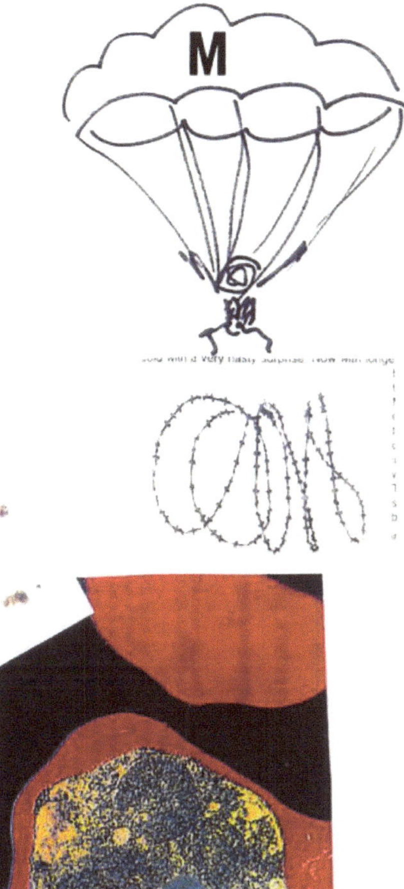

X

The quick browN fox jumps over the lazy dog.
Uif rvjdl cspxO gpy kvnqt pwfs uif mbaz eph.
Vjg swkem dTqyp hrz lworu qxgt vjg ncba fqi.
Wkh txlfn eurzq iSa mxpsv ryhu wkh odcb grj.
Xli uymgO fvsar jtb nyrtw sziv xli pedc hsk.
Ymj vznhp gwtbs kuc ozsux tAjw ymj qfed itl.
Znk waoiq hxuCt lvd patvy ubkx znk rgfe jum.
Aol xbpjr iyvdu mwe qbuwz vcly aol sHgf kvn.
Bpm ycqks jzwev nxf rcvxa wdmz bpm tIhg lwo.
Cqn zdrLt kaxfw oyg sdwyb xena cqn ujih mxp.
Dro aesmu Lbygy pzh texzc yfob dro vkji nyq.
Esp bftnv mczhz qai wfyad zgpc Esp wlkj ozr.
Ftq cguow ndaia rbj xgzbe ahqd ftq xmlk paS.
Gur dhvpx oebjb sck yhAcf cite eur znml qbt.
Hvs eiwqy pfckc tdl zibdg djuf fvs aoNm rcu.
Iwt fjxrz qgdld uem ajceh ekvg gwt bpon sDv.
Jxu gkysa rheme vfn bkdfi flwh hxu cqpo Tew.
Kyv Hlztb isfnf wgo clej gmxi iyv drqp ufx.
Lzw imauc jtgog xhp dmfk hnyj jzw Esrq vgy.
Max jnbvd kuhph yiq engl iozk kax fTsr whz.
Nby kocwe lviqi zjr fOhm jpal lby guts xia.
Ocz lpdxf mwjRj aks gpin kqbm mcz hvut yjb.
Pda mqeyg nxksk bIT hqjo lrcn nda iwvu zkc.
Qeb nrfzh oyltl cmu irkp msdO oeb jxyv ald.
Rfc osgaI pzmum dnv jslq ntep pfc kyzw bme.
Sgd pthbj qanvn eow ktmr oudq qgd lzax cnf.

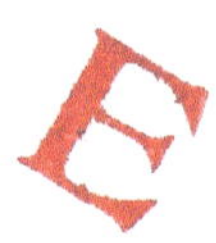

<table>
<tr><td>abuse</td><td align="right">caress</td></tr>
<tr><td>assault</td><td align="right">clasp</td></tr>
<tr><td>attack</td><td align="right">coddle</td></tr>
<tr><td>coerce</td><td align="right">comfort</td></tr>
<tr><td>convulse</td><td align="right">cuddle</td></tr>
<tr><td>disfigure</td><td align="right">delight</td></tr>
<tr><td>frighten</td><td align="right">embrace</td></tr>
<tr><td>horrify</td><td align="right">enrapture</td></tr>
<tr><td>hurt</td><td align="right">fondle</td></tr>
<tr><td>injure</td><td align="right">gratify</td></tr>
<tr><td>intimidate</td><td align="right">hug</td></tr>
<tr><td>maltreat</td><td align="right">mollify</td></tr>
<tr><td colspan="2">rapebatterscrewfucksuckniplickkiss</td></tr>
<tr><td>rip</td><td align="right">nuzzle</td></tr>
<tr><td>slash</td><td align="right">pat</td></tr>
<tr><td>strike</td><td align="right">pet</td></tr>
<tr><td>terrorize</td><td align="right">pleasure</td></tr>
<tr><td>thrash</td><td align="right">smoothe</td></tr>
<tr><td>torment</td><td align="right">soothe</td></tr>
<tr><td>wound</td><td align="right">stroke</td></tr>
</table>

The Marriage of Heaven and Hell

Every line I write here has been stricken out because I know before I ever begin writing anything no matter what that my first draft will never survive looking at again. There is therefore no reason to save it except as a reminder of how I began whatever it was I intended to write; besides, if I save it I might mistake it for a later version and go over it once again anyway. My beginning I prefer to forget, better yet not to keep unless crossing them out may turn it into a relic.

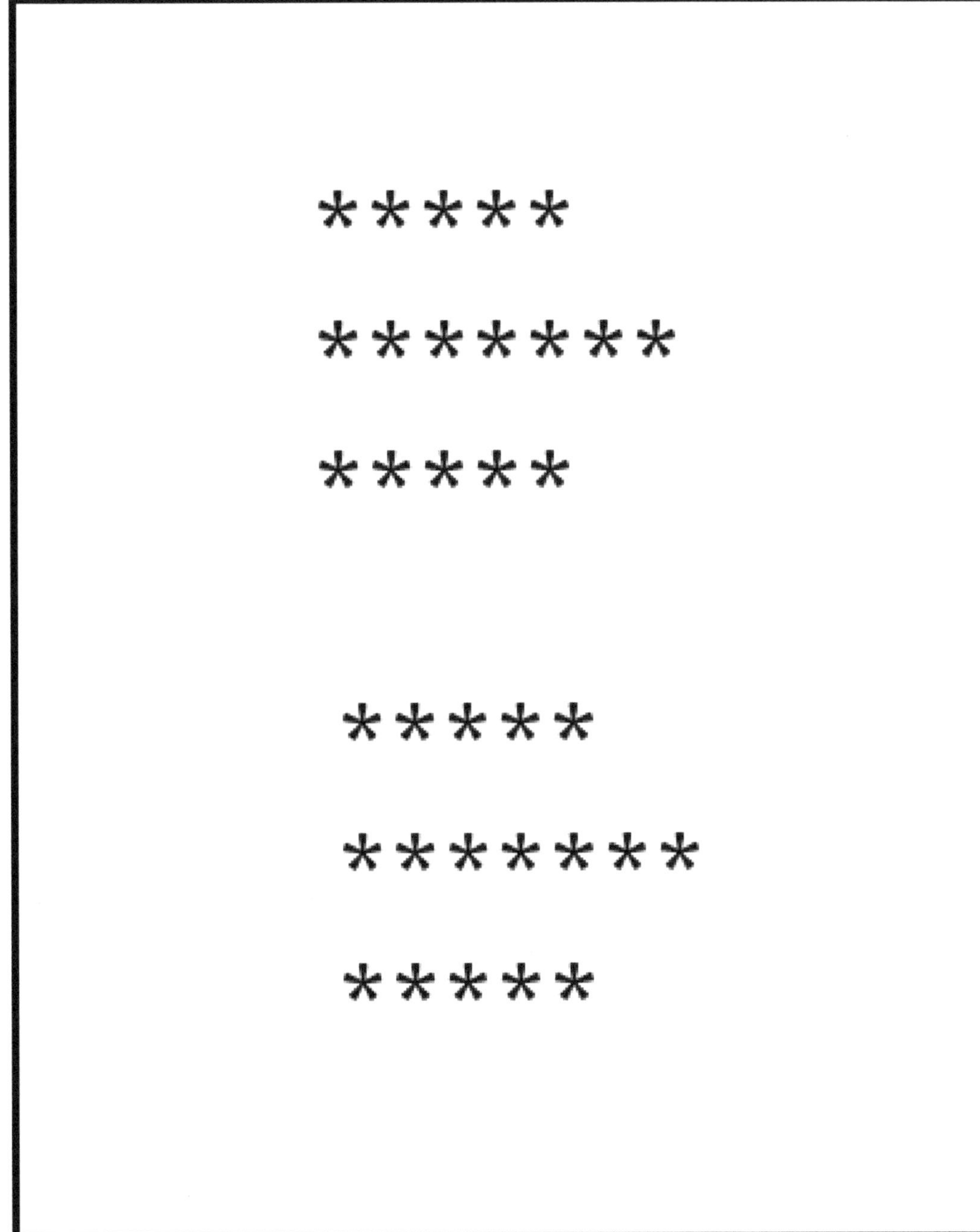

DOUBLE HAIKU PASSWORDS

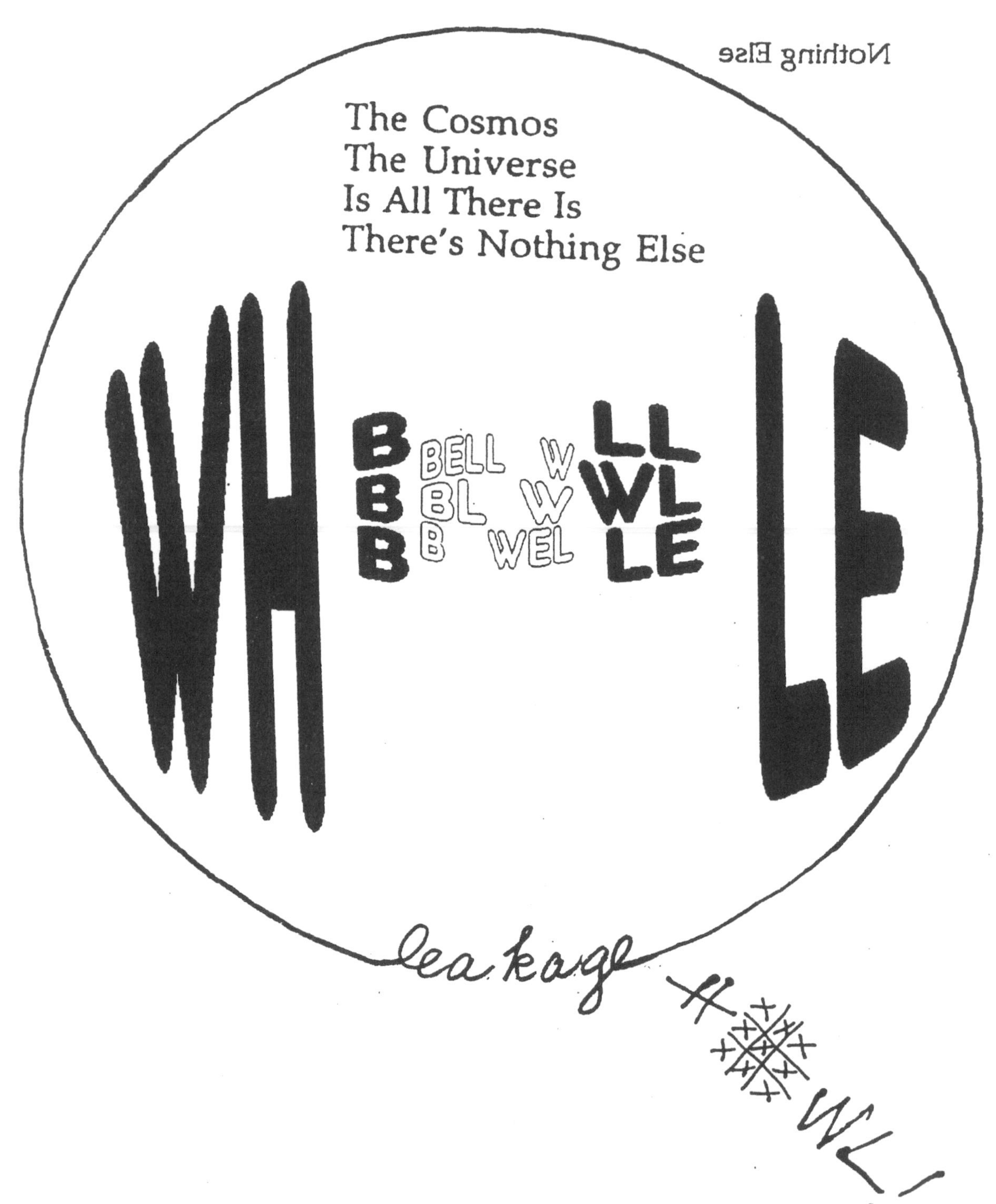
Nothing Else
The Cosmos
The Universe
Is All There Is
There's Nothing Else
WH
B BELL W LL
B BL W WL
B B WEL LE
LE
leakage
H WL!

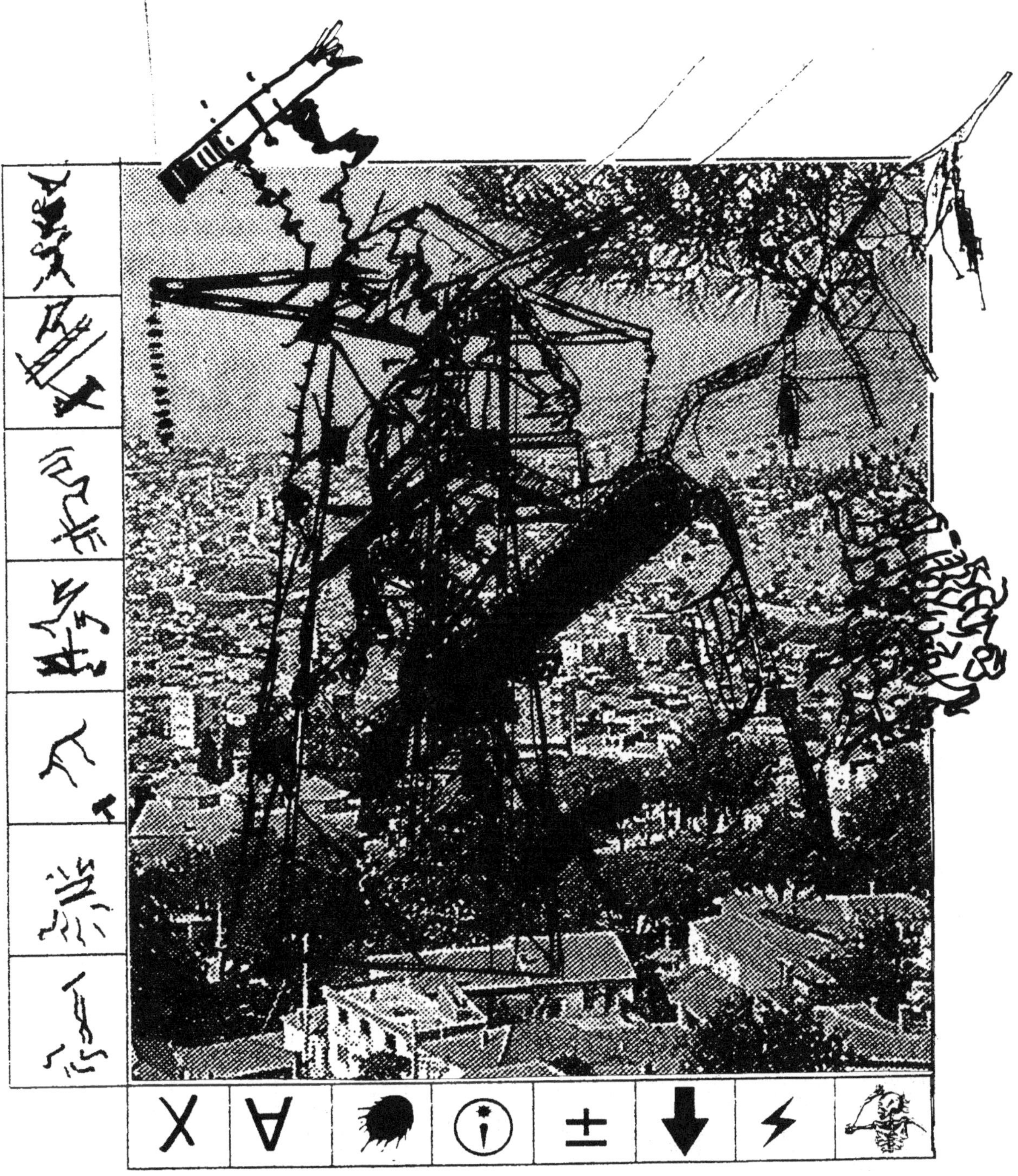

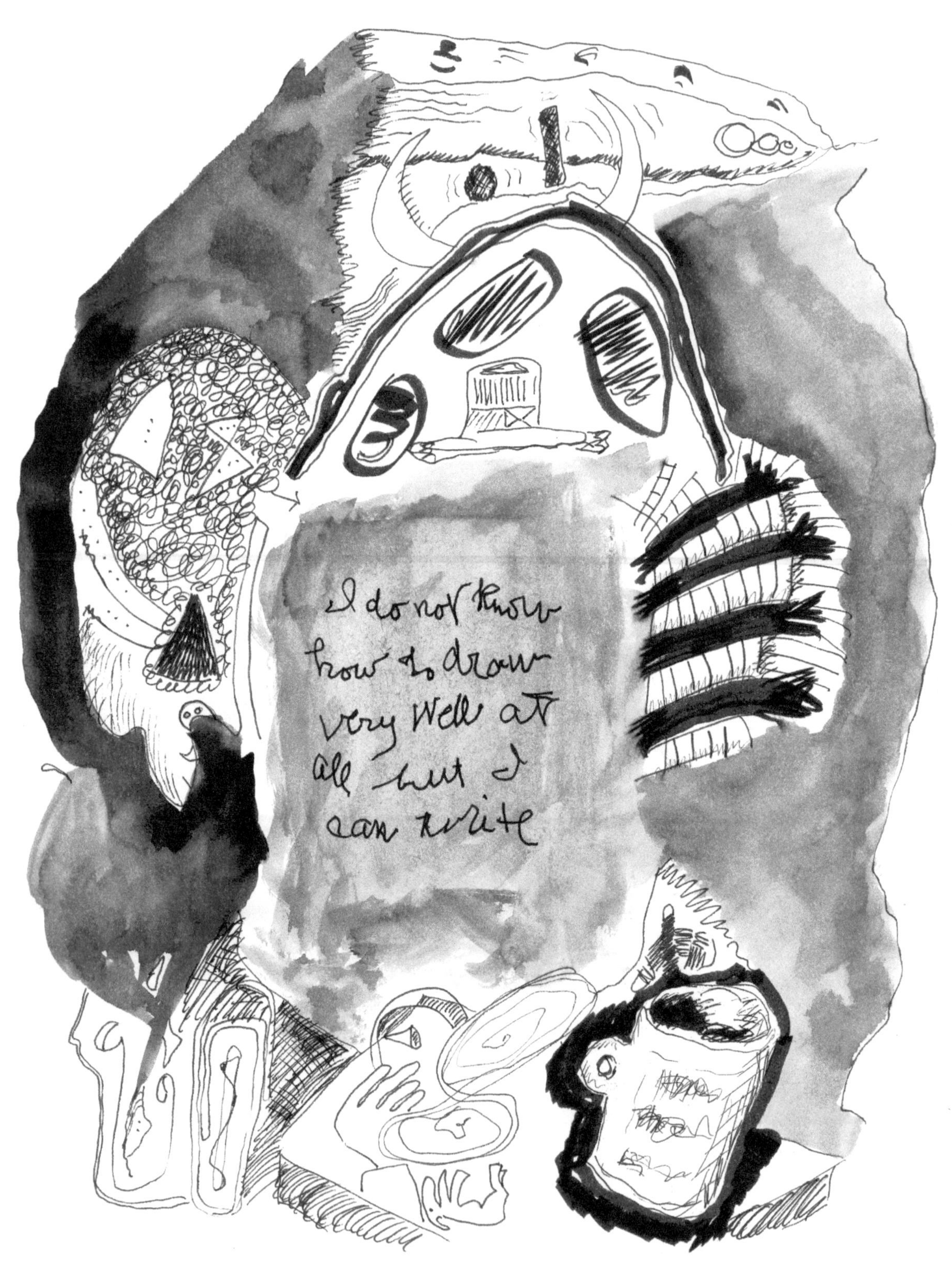
I do not know
how to draw
very well at
all but I
can write

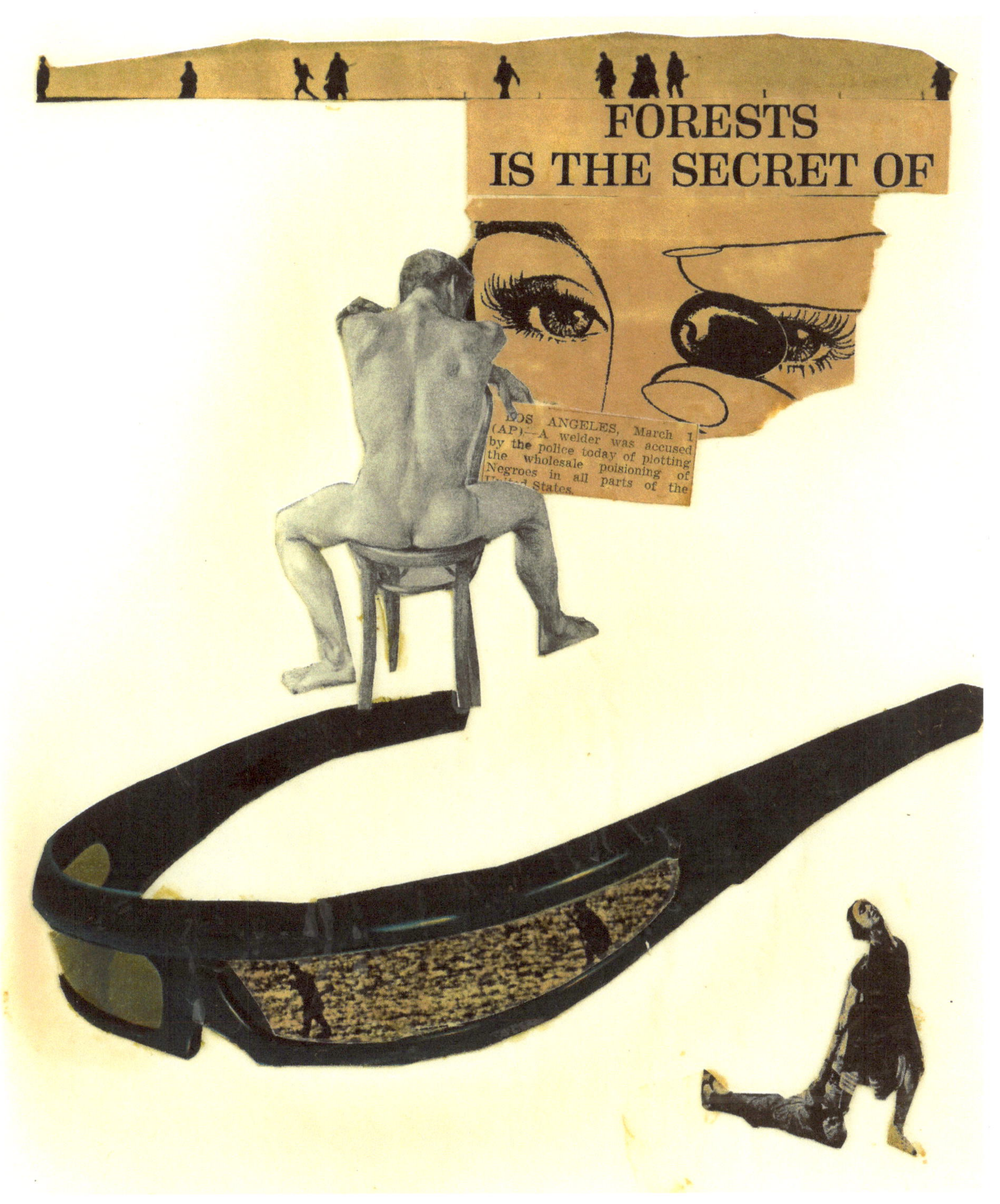
FORESTS
IS THE SECRET OF
LOS ANGELES, March 1
(AP)—A welder was accused
by the police today of plotting
the wholesale poisioning of
Negroes in all parts of the
States.

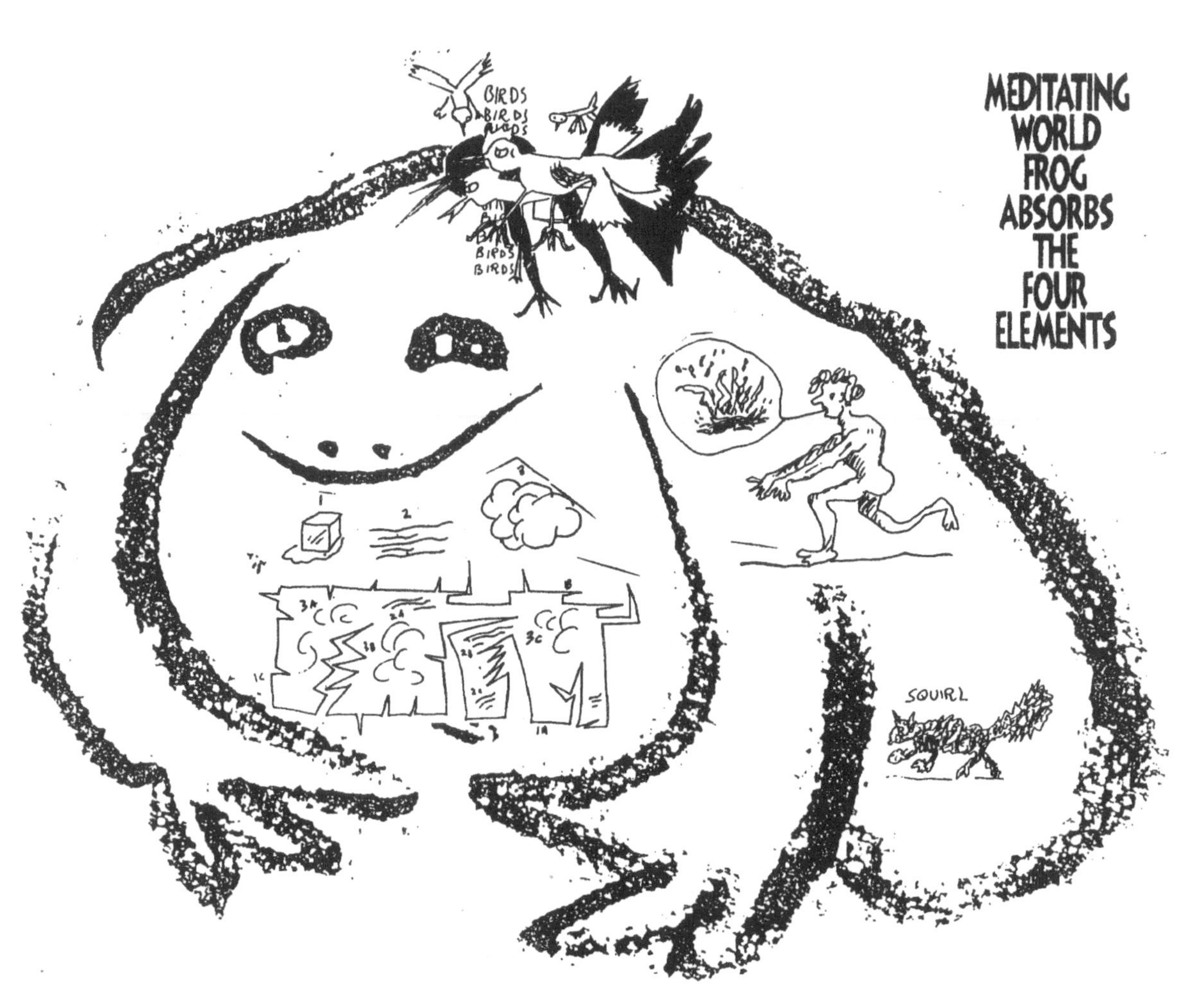
MEDITATING WORLD FROG ABSORBS THE FOUR ELEMENTS
BIRDS
BIRDS
BIRDS
BIRDS
BIRDS
SQUIRL

disappoit

Old Mother Hubba
Went to the cupb
To fetch her poor d
But when she cam
The cupboard was
And so the poor dot

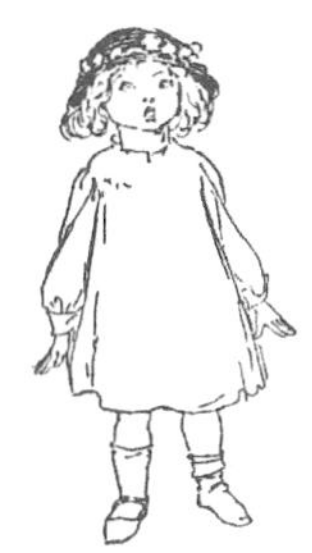

Tom, Tom, the pipe
Stole a pig and aw
The pig was eat, a
Till he ran cryint

Jack and Jill
Went up the hill,
To fetch a pail of wa
Jack fell down
And broke his crown,
And Jill came tumblit

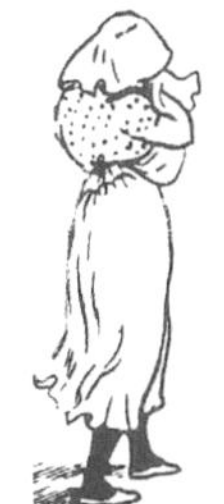

Cock a doodle do
My Dame has lost
My Master's lost
And knows not wt

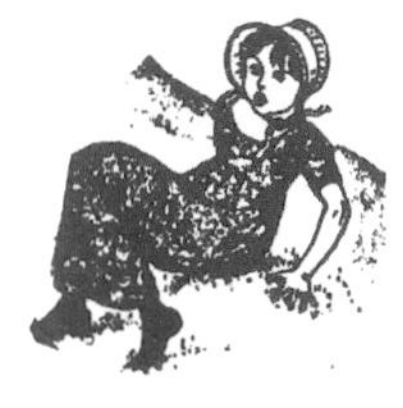

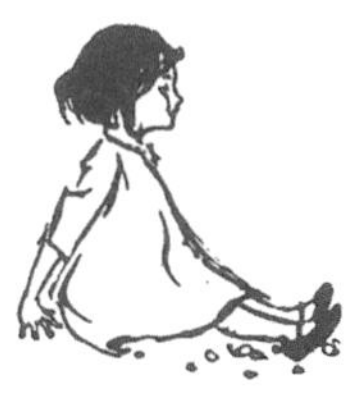

Little Miss Muf
Sat on a tuffet
Eating her c
Along came a sp
And sat down bt

Little Boy Blue, co
The cow's in the me
But where is the li
He's under the hays
Will you wake him?
For if I do he's st

Little Tom Tucke
Sings for his su
What shall he ea
White bread and
How will he cut
Without any knif
And how will he
Without any wift

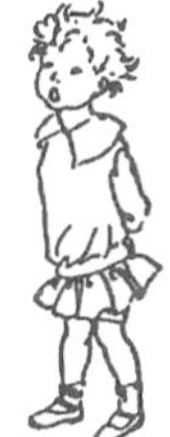

to swallow bile

to defile altar

to lap sluice

to inflame wound

to cast evil eye

to covet flesh

to unman Saturn

to mutilate doll

to dangle filth

to engorge member

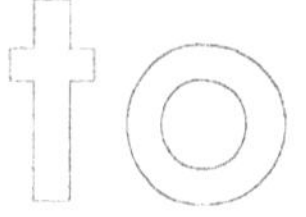

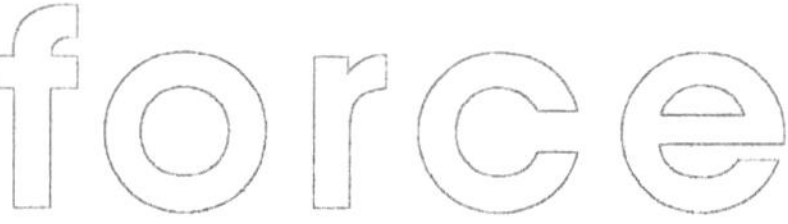

to bind Isaac

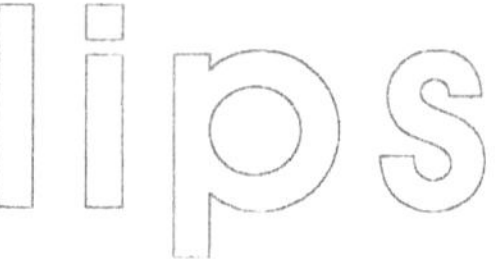

to fig God

to wean brat

to finger hole

to drain drop

to topple icon

to foul source

to incite mob

to ravish Sabine

to unearth corpse

to mount imbecile to

interrupt

Onan

to entrap stranger

to strike mother

to drill cranium

TO FONDLE TRIGGER

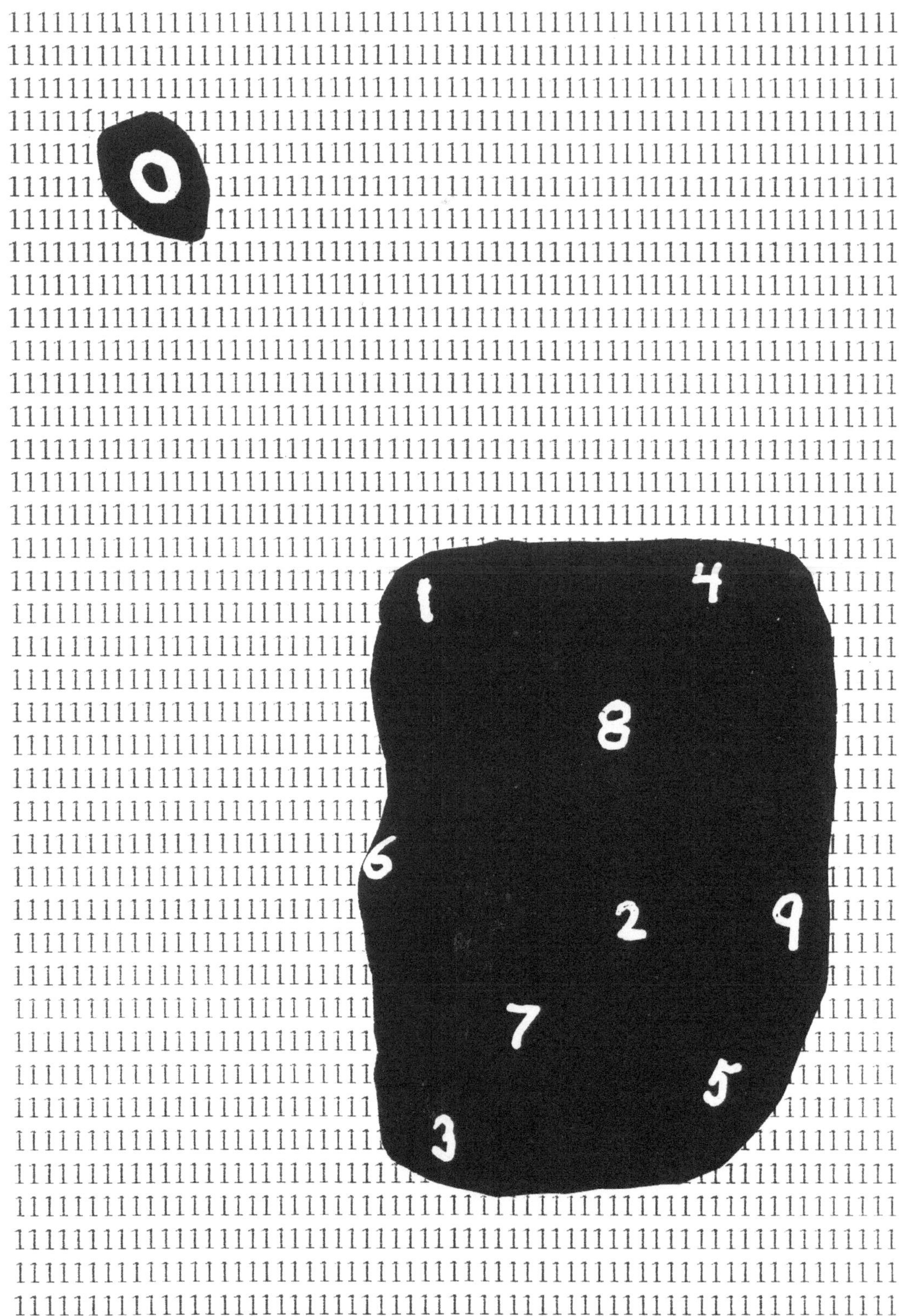

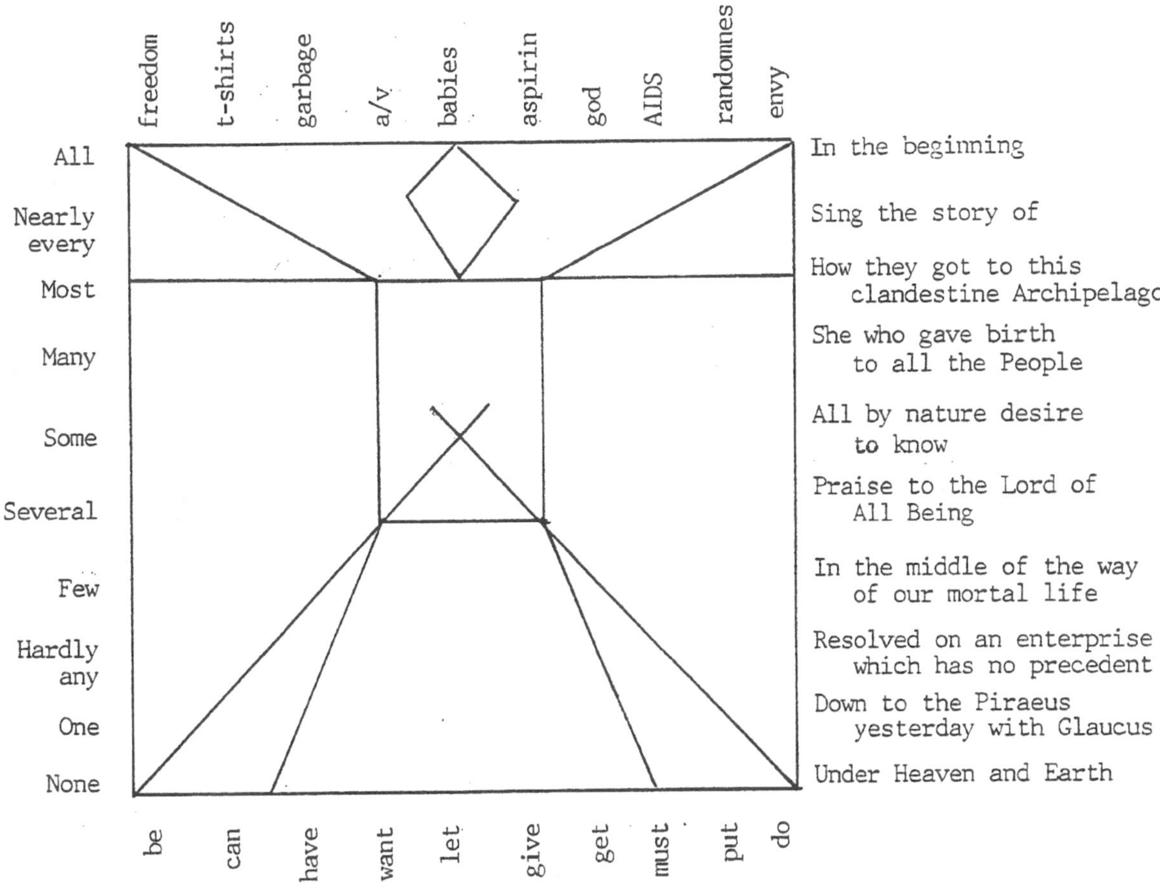
freedom
t-shirts
garbage
a/v
babies
aspirin
god
AIDS
randomnes
envy
All
Nearly every
Most
Many
Some
Several
Few
Hardly any
One
None
In the beginning
Sing the story of
How they got to this clandestine Archipelago
She who gave birth to all the People
All by nature desire to know
Praise to the Lord of All Being
In the middle of the way of our mortal life
Resolved on an enterprise which has no precedent
Down to the Piraeus yesterday with Glaucus
Under Heaven and Earth
be
can
have
want
let
give
get
must
put
do

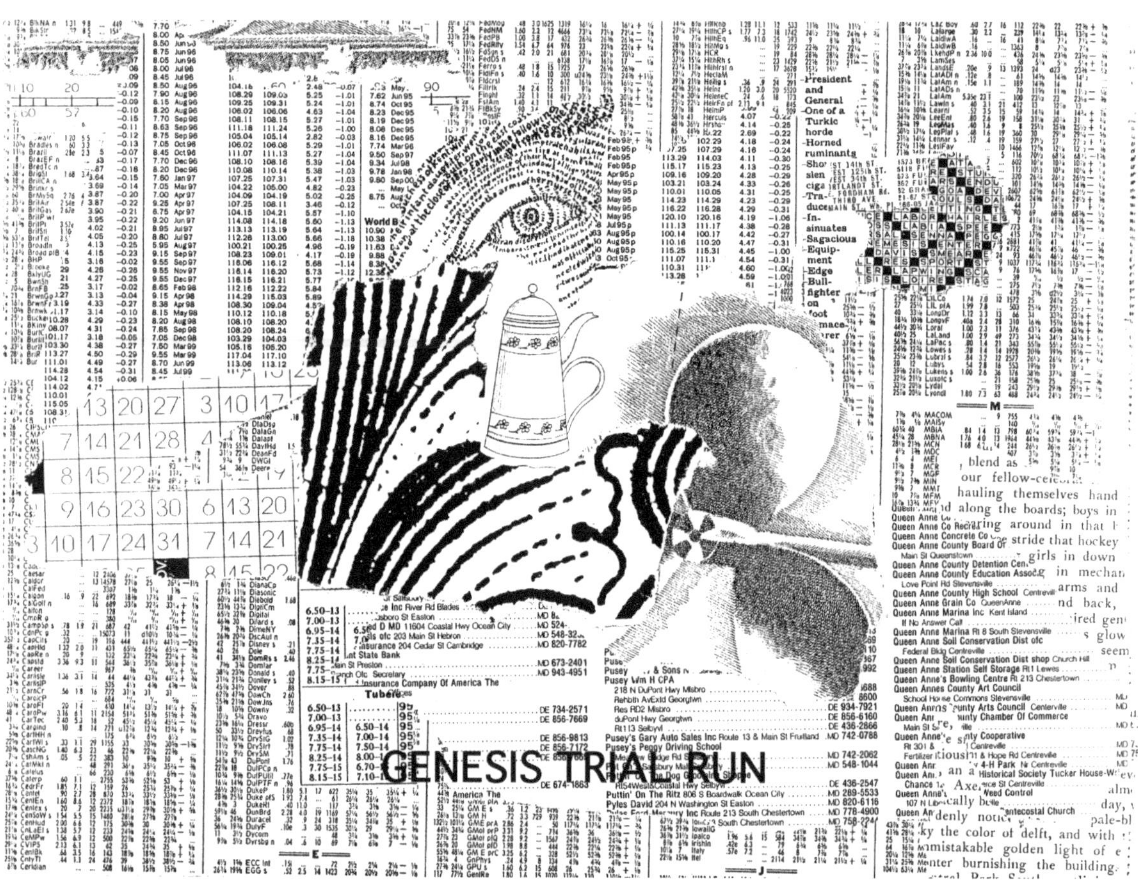
GENESIS TRIAL RUN

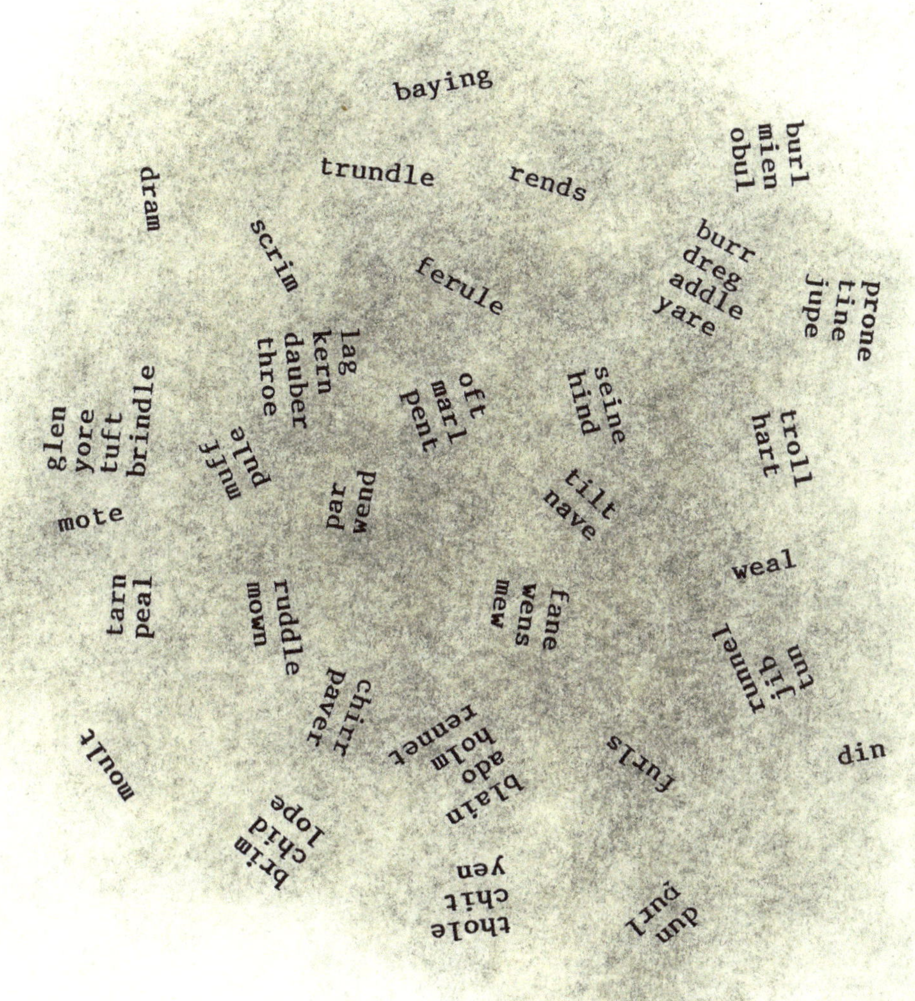

GLOAM ZONE

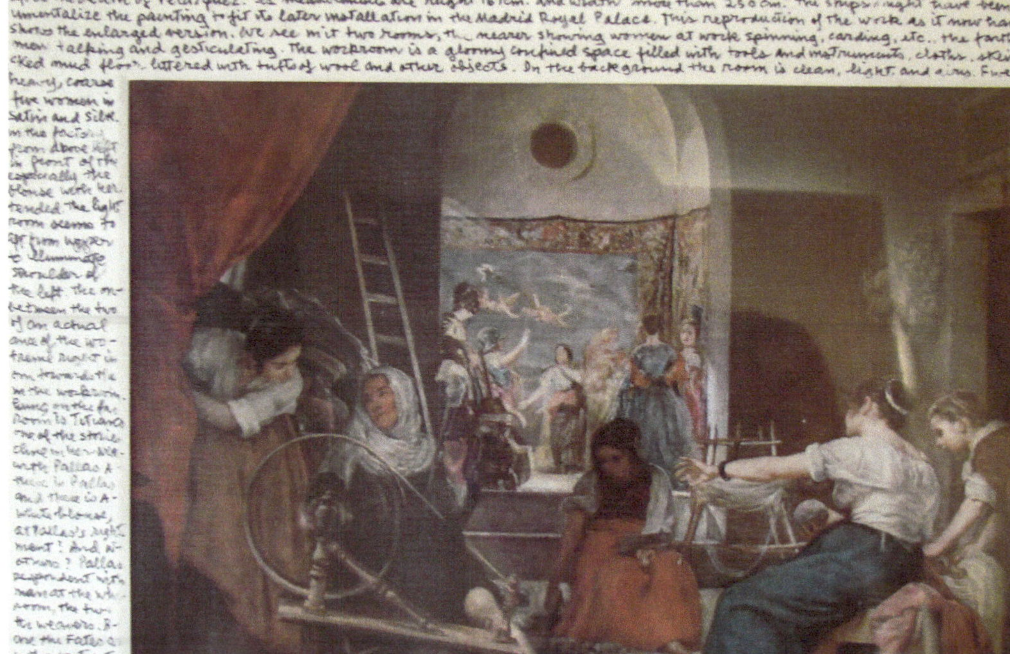

On First Seeing Las Hilanderas

(nesslessnesslessness)

endocitra
cis
hamakata
perimethog
supra
pro
umbeza
semidemi
preter
proso
sinemetahypo
intel
embiskata
col
ama
af
ag
y
twi
seso
omainon
M
n
epiljuxta
leu
anananananananaf
benepr
intusecpor*uh*. . . . .*mmmmm*exterohypter
over
la
contredede
pilcol
utter
v
sysu
triretro
negnon
amabene
s
ogpil
intro
forfor
prodsum
*uhwello*pisthopiso

oonoonsterurient

arityoriousyanohwhutmsayn?

hoodixityendumdom*like—right?*

tresuloseysm

oideanacle

trixitude

wardxion***youdig***?

tionosityurishnessity

origins

2 S

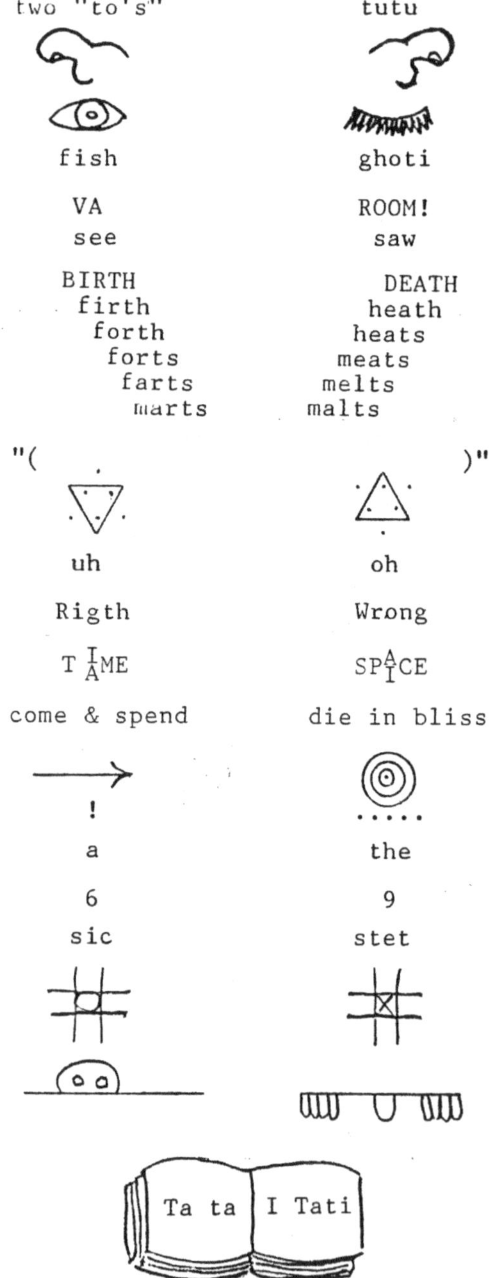
two "to's"
tutu
fish
ghoti
VA
ROOM!
see
saw
BIRTH
firth
forth
forts
farts
marts
DEATH
heath
heats
meats
melts
malts
"(
)"
uh
oh
Rigth
Wrong
T I A ME
SP A I CE
come & spend
die in bliss
!
a
the
6
9
sic
stet
Ta ta I Tati

Obscurity, My One-in-Three Piece-Together Fate:
Original Manuscript by Weiss Out of Wyatt

Stond who so list up
of courtes estates, and rejoyce;
and use me quyet without or stoppe,
unknowen in courte, that hath suche brackish joye
In hidden place, so lette my dayes forthe passe,
when my yeares be done, withouten noyse,
ay dye aged, after the common trace
death greep' the right hand by the crop
at is moche knowen of other; and of him
oth dye unknowen, dazed with dreadf

who so list upon the slipper toppe
courtes estates, and lette me heare rejoyce;
use me quyet without lett or stoppe,
knowen in courte, that hath suche brackish
n hidden place, so lette my dayes forth
when my yeares be done, withouten noys
may dye aged, after the common trace
n death greep' the right hand by the croppe
at is moche knowen of other; and of him self alas,
Doth dye unknowen, dazed with dreadfull face.

nd who so list upon the slipper toppe
courtes estates, and lette me heare rejoyce;
use me quyet without lett or stoppe,
Unknowen in courte, that hath such brackish joyes:
In hidden place, so lette my dayes forthe passe,
That when my yeares be done, withouten noysse
I may dye aged after the common trace
For hym death greep' the right hand by the
That is muche knowen of other; and of
Doth dye unknowen, dazed with dre

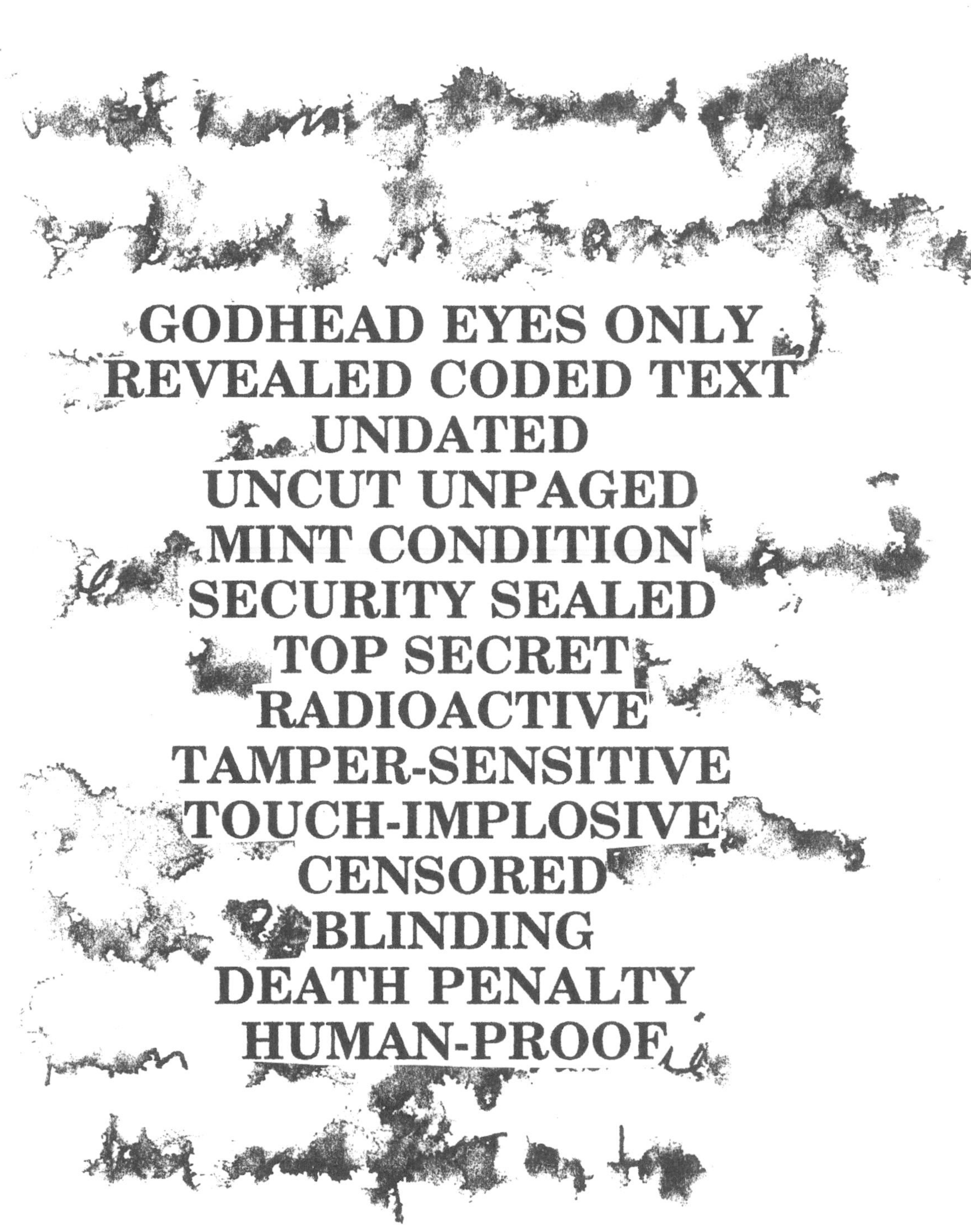
GODHEAD EYES ONLY
REVEALED CODED TEXT
UNDATED
UNCUT UNPAGED
MINT CONDITION
SECURITY SEALED
TOP SECRET
RADIOACTIVE
TAMPER-SENSITIVE
TOUCH-IMPLOSIVE
CENSORED
BLINDING
DEATH PENALTY
HUMAN-PROOF

Hand Over Everything You've Got

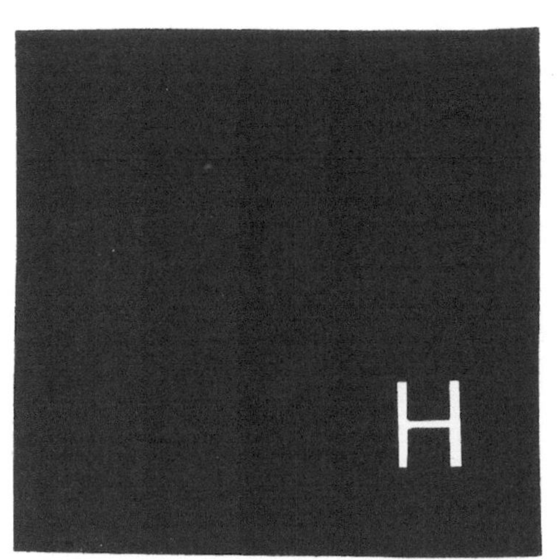

Why the World Is Not the Case

When you do something and it doesn't
workout
You may decide you won't go on
And you'll either give up
Or try a little longer just a little longer
One way or another
Until it becomes clear
When it's all over that it's all over
But not whether you gave up entirely
Or only gave up trying

WITE BOX

BLAC. BOX

Notes

1. Black box with white "H."
2. Black box subtitled "WITE BOX with arrow pointing to white box.
3. Black box also secondarily subtitled "BLAC. BOX."
4. White box interrupted by handwritten poem entitled "Why the World Is Not the Case."
5. The "BLAC." of #3 above apparently an abbreviation.
6. Notes listed here as above and including this item, all entitled "Notes."

alivaaniesapaucecabcabiescaldcalecaldcalecallchmearcoodyncori
acourcrancratchcratchingcrudcruffcrungecudcumcurfcurvyeborrhe
aebumecretionedimentepsiserpigoerumewagehithmeerhmutzhpritzla
glaverlimelobberloploughludgeluicelurplurrylushmearmirchmooch
mudgemutmutchnotoilootopordesoreousepatterpeckpermpewpillpill
agepilthpitpittleplashplatplatterplutterpotpoutprayprinklepum
epunkpurtputumtewtigmaullywabweatwillalivaaniesapaucecabcabie
scaldcalecaldcalecallchmearcoodyncoria[illegible]atchcratching
crudcruffcrungecudcumcurfcurvyebor[illegible]edimentepsi
serpigoerumewagehithmeerhmutzhprit[illegible]rloplough
ludgeluicelurplurrylushmear[illegible]ilootop
ordesoreousepatterpeckper[illegible]shpl
atplatterplutterpotpout[illegible]maul
lywabweatwillalivaani[illegible]chm
earcoodyncoriacourcr[illegible]ratchingcrudcr[illegible]ur
fcurvyeborrheaebume[illegible]mentepsiserpig[illegible]er
hmutzhpritzlaglaver[illegible]loploughludgelu[illegible]m
earmirchmoochmudge[illegible]toi[illegible]topordesor[illegible]pe
rmpewpillpillagepi[illegible]tp
rayprinklepumepu[illegible]esa
paucecabcabiescaldca[illegible]mear[illegible]yncoria[illegible]ancr
atchcratchingcrudcruf[illegible]eborrheaebumecreti
onedimentepsiserpigoerume[illegible]itzlaglaverlimel
obberloploughludgeluicelurp[illegible]oochmudgemutmut
chnotoilootopordesoreousepatterpe[illegible]llagepilthpit
pittleplashplatplatterplutterpotp[illegible]epumepunkpurtpu
tumtewtigmaullywabweatwillalivaaniesapauc[illegible]abie[illegible]aldcaleca
ldcalecallchmearcoodyncoriacourcrancrat[illegible]udcruffcr
ungecudcumcurfcurvyeborrheaebumecretio[illegible]pigoerum
ewagehithmeerhmutzhpritzlaglaverlimelob[illegible]geluicel
urplurrylushmearmirchmoochmudgemutmutchn[illegible]rdesoreous
epatterpeckpermpewpillpillagepilthpitpi[illegible]platterpl
utterpotpoutprayprinklepumepunkpurtput[illegible]ywabweatwi
llalivaaniesapaucecabcabiescaldcale[illegible]mearcoodynco
riacourcrancratchcratchingcrudcruffcr[illegible]urfcurvyeborr
hea[illegible]retionedimentepsiserpigoeru[illegible]eerhmutzhpritz
lag[illegible]lobberloploughludgelui[illegible]lushmearmirchmoo
chmu[illegible]ilootopordesore[illegible]ckpermpewpillpi
llage[illegible]ashplatplatte[illegible]otpoutprayprinklep
umepun[illegible]igmaully[illegible]ivaaniesapaucecabcab
iescald[illegible]allch[illegible]acourcrancratchcratchi
ngcrudcr[illegible]eaebumecretionedimentep
siserpigo[illegible]aglaverlimelobberloplou
ghludgelu[illegible]chmudgemutmutchnotoiloot
opordesoreousep[illegible]pillagepilthpitpittleplash
platplatterplutter[illegible]epumepunkpurtputumtewtigma
ullywabweatwillal[illegible]esapaucecabcabiescaldcalecaldcalecallc
hmearcoodyncoriacourcrancratchcratchingcrudcruffcrungecudcumc
urfcurvyeborrheaebumecretionedimentepsiserpigoerumewagehithme
erhmutzhpritzlaglaverlimelobberloploughludgeluicelurplurrylus
hmearmirchmoochmudgemutmutchnotoilootopordesoreousepatterpeck
permpewpillpillagepilthpialivaaniesapaucecabcabiescaldcalecal
dcalecallchmearcoodyncoriacourcrancratchcratchingcrudcruffcru
ngecudcumcurfcurvyeborrheaebumecretionedimentepsiserpigoerume

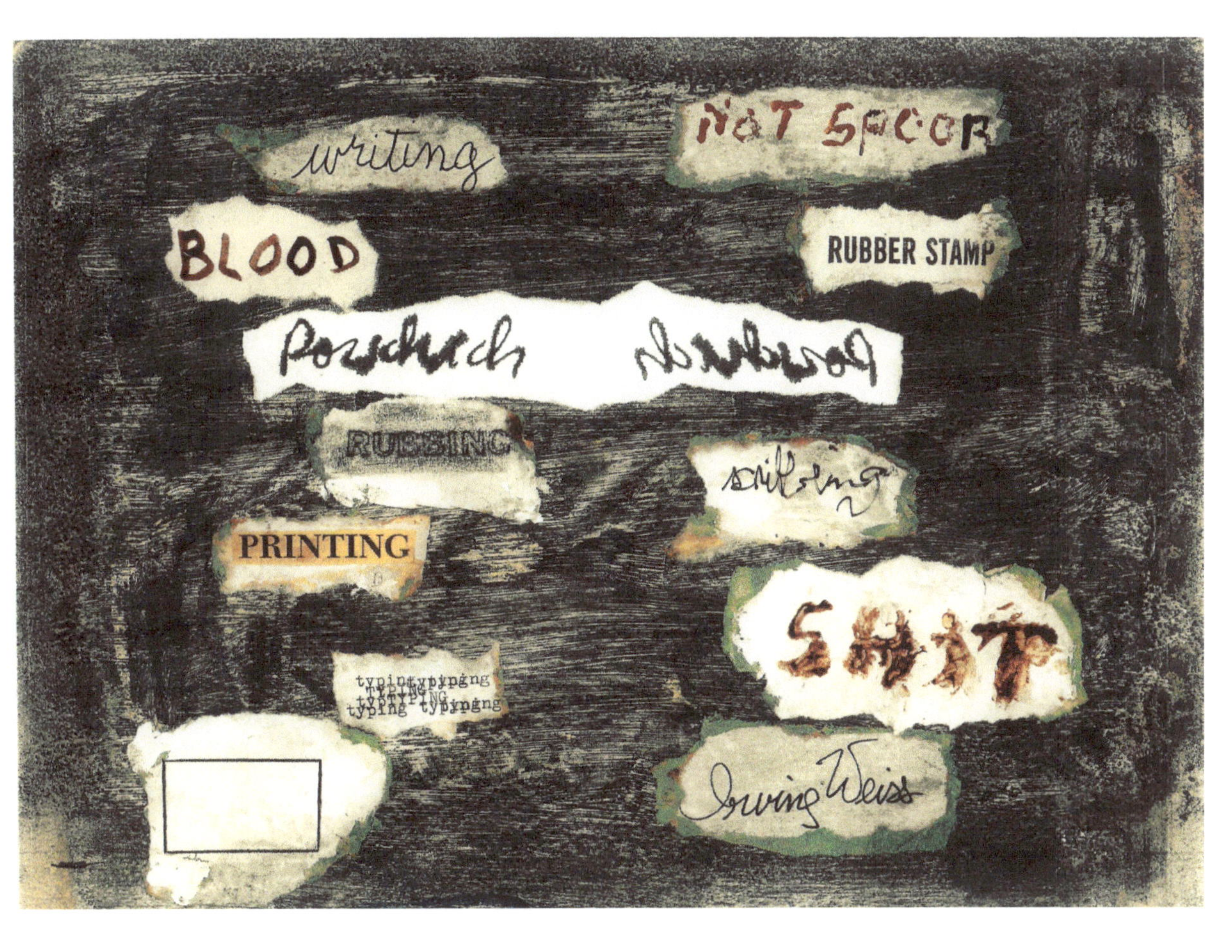
writing
BLOOD
RUBBER STAMP
RUBBING
PRINTING
SHIT
Irving Weiss

* This asterisk unauthorized by any text proper the presence of whose content is marked by its concrete avoidance of visibility identifiable only as nowhere on the page is intended to indicate an apparently absolutely minimal piece of text in the blank space above.

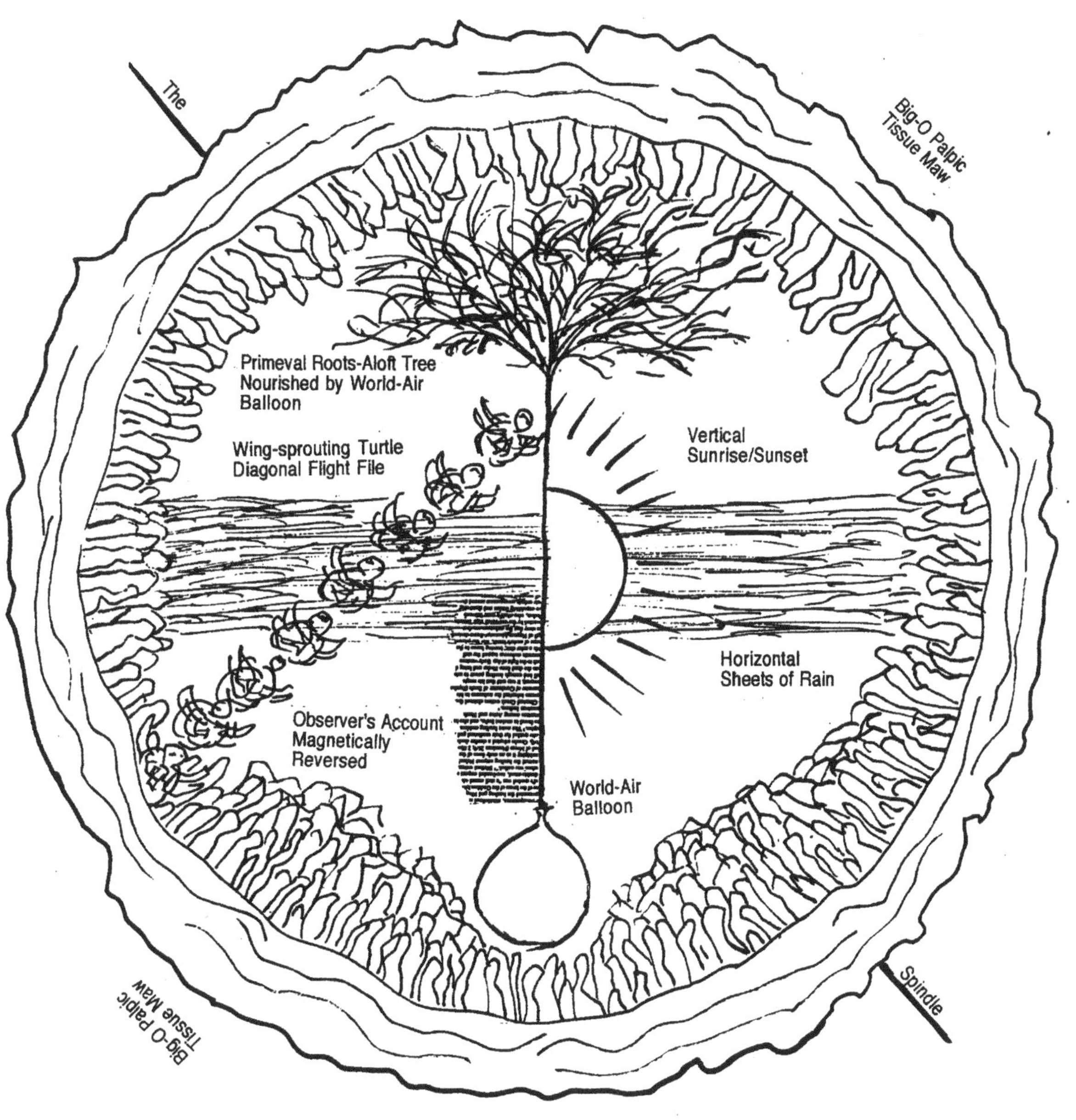
The
Big-O Palpic
Tissue Maw
Primeval Roots-Aloft Tree
Nourished by World-Air
Balloon
Wing-sprouting Turtle
Diagonal Flight File
Vertical
Sunrise/Sunset
Horizontal
Sheets of Rain
Observer's Account
Magnetically
Reversed
World-Air
Balloon
Big-O Palpic
Tissue Maw
Spindle

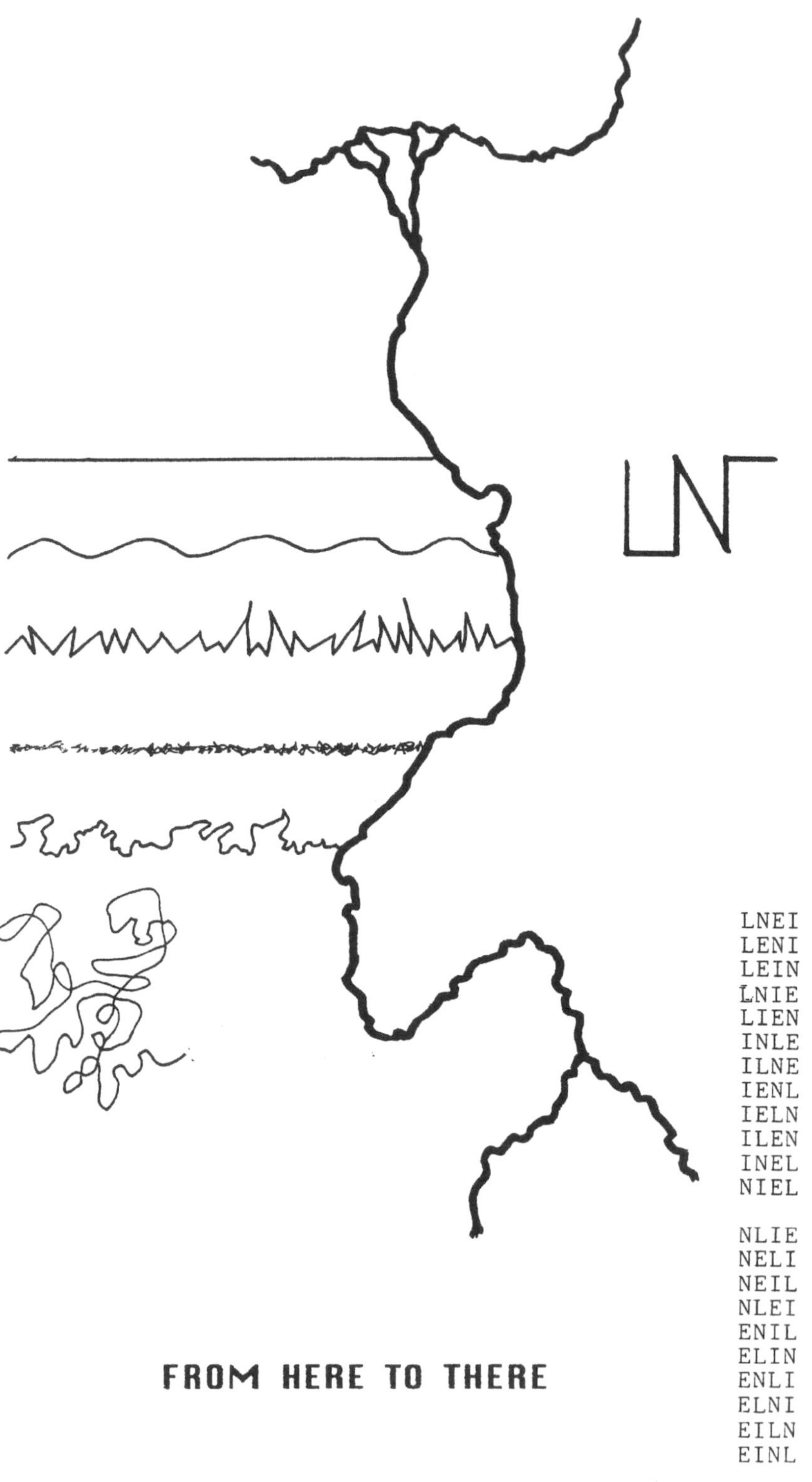
LNEI
LENI
LEIN
LNIE
LIEN
INLE
ILNE
IENL
IELN
ILEN
INEL
NIEL
NLIE
NELI
NEIL
NLEI
ENIL
ELIN
ENLI
ELNI
EILN
EINL
FROM HERE TO THERE

FULL FRONTAL VIEW

FULL REAR VIEW

PROFILE

HEADFIRST

PROFILE

H U N R E K

PRONE

SUPINE

Vertical Reality Sandwich

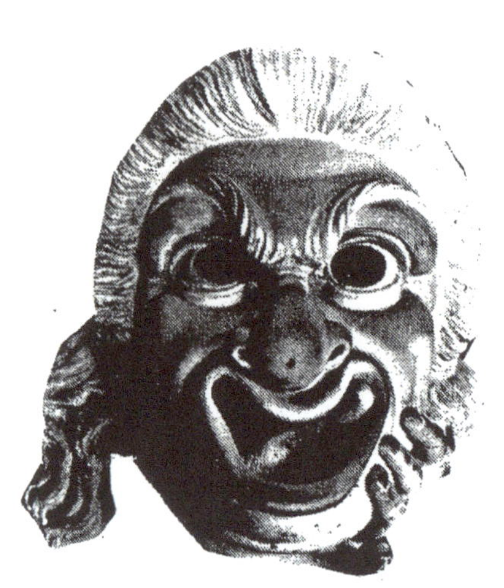

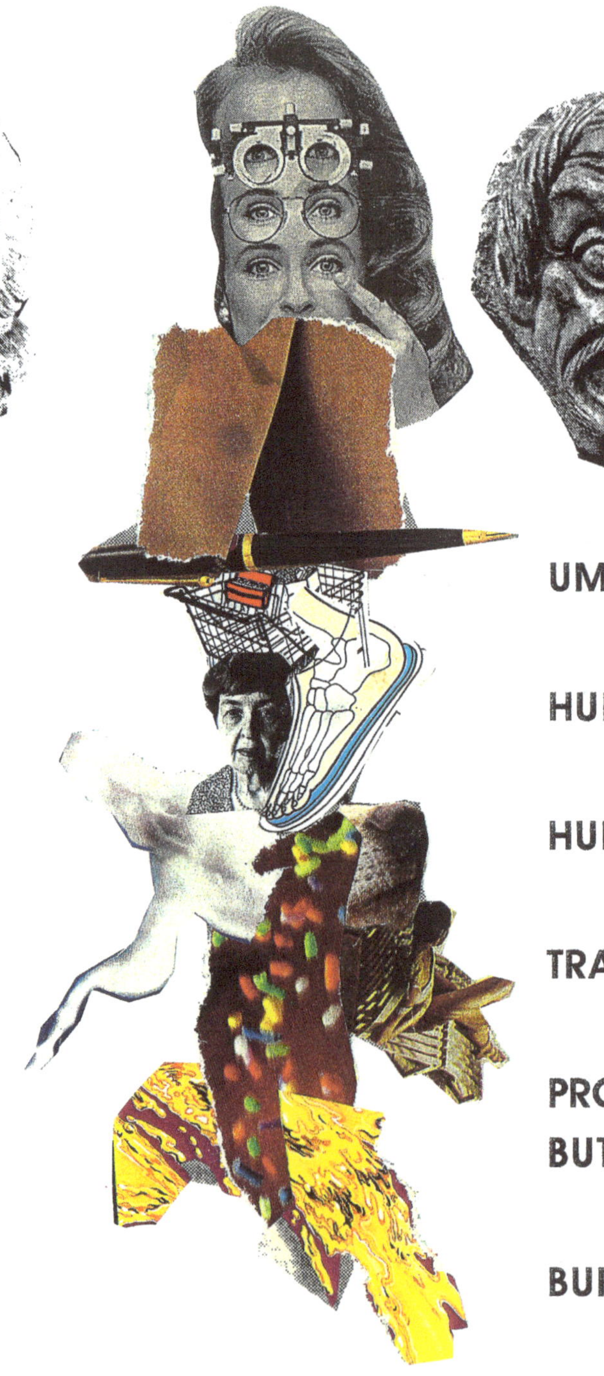

MELON SLICE

HAMMOCK

SAUCER

GONDOLA

CUPPED HAND

CRADLE

UMBRELLA

HUMMOCK

HUNCHBACK

TRAJECTORY

PRONE BUTTOCK

BURIAL VAULT

WATAR

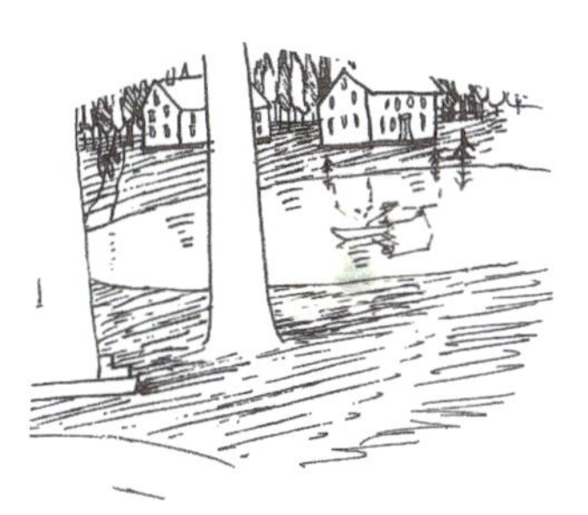

P O O D

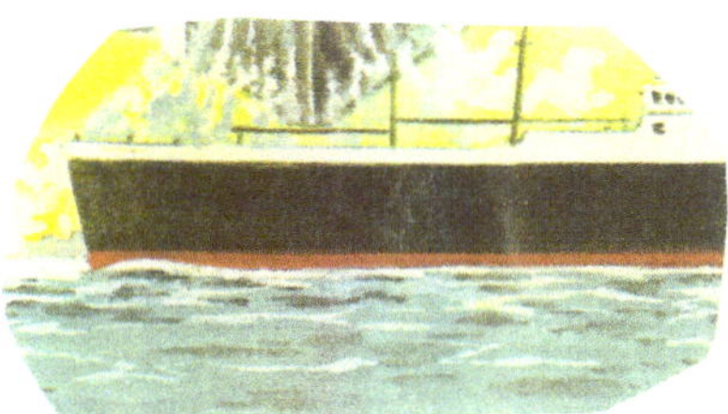

O C E A M

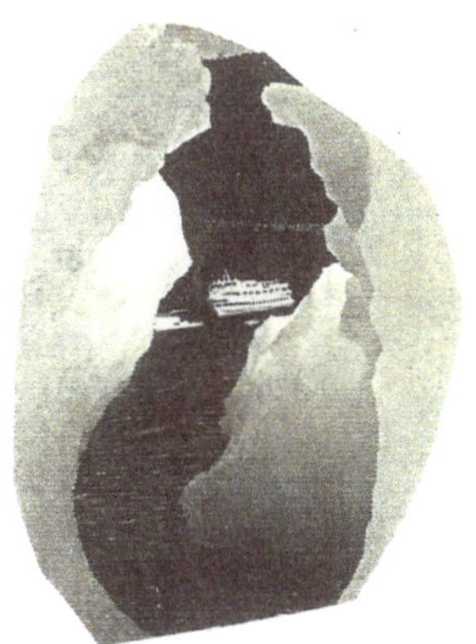

F J O R G

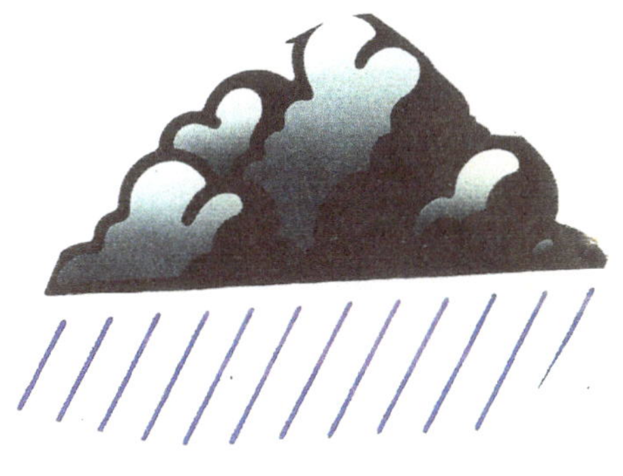

C R O U D S

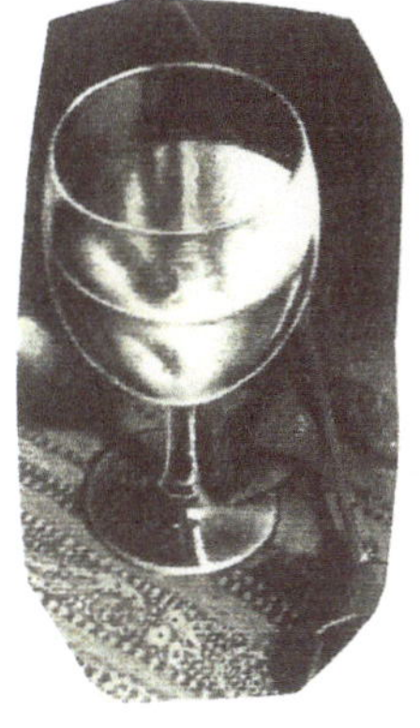

D R I N E

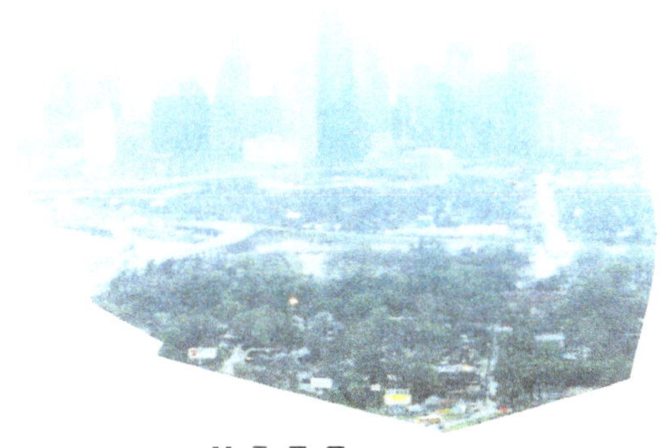

M I F T

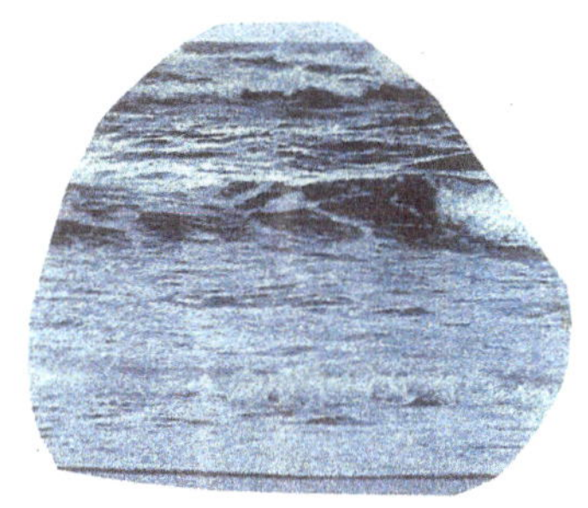

W A B E S

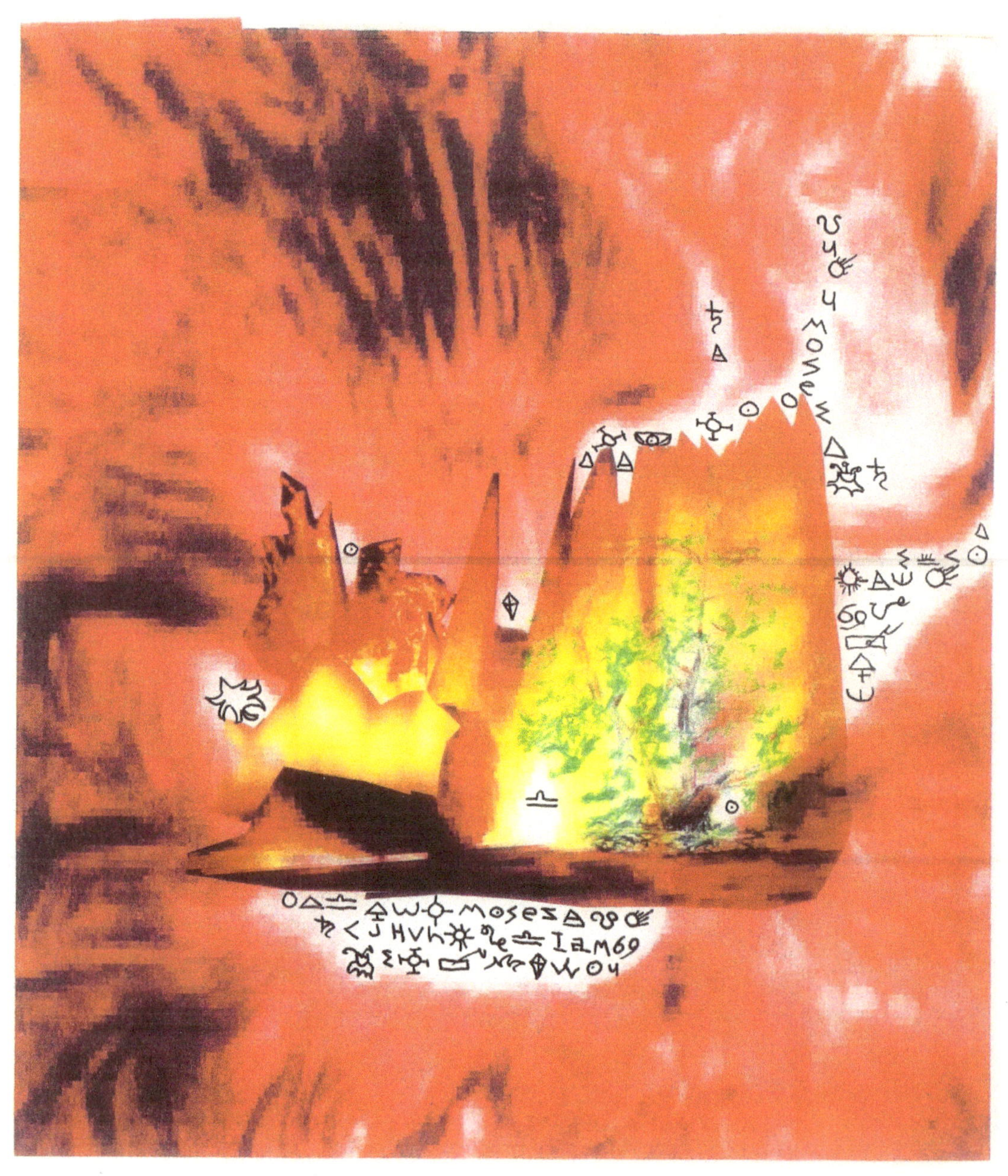

MOISHE! MOISHE!

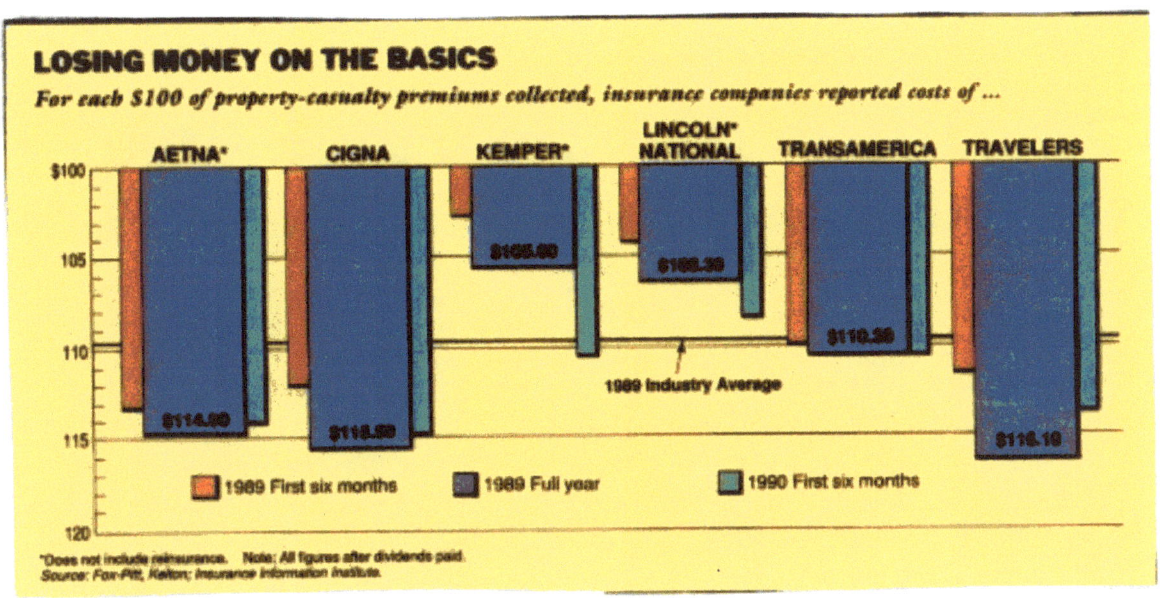

O may I with myself agree,
And never covet what I see.
Content me with an humble shade,
My passions tam'd, my wishes laid;
For while our wishes wildly roll,
We banish quiet from the soul:
'Tis thus the busy beat the air;
And misers gather wealth and care.

Now, ev'n now, my joys run high,
As on the mountain turf I lie;
While the wanton zephyr sings,
And in the vale perfumes his wings;
While the waters murmur deep;
While the shepherd charms his sheep;
While the birds unbounded fly,
And with musick fill the sky,
Now, ev'n now, my joys run high.

—John Dyer, from *Grongar Hill*

ЯƎVƎNEER LEVE REVEAL LEVER RELIEVE LEAVER

CROOK STRAI(GH)T QUƎER

why bother to ask where this line is going

not a question
the above words made a statement
this line may be safely ignored

there is no need for any other lines

any line forgives any other line:
THE BOREDOM OF REDUNDANCY
(the shimmering light at the center of boredom)

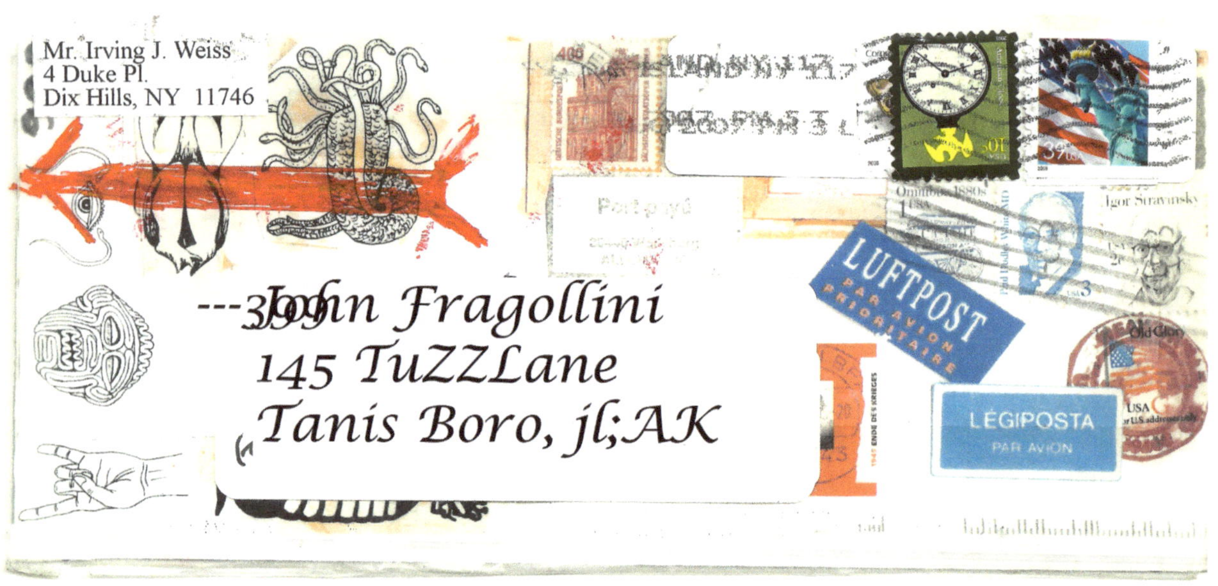
Mr. Irving J. Weiss
4 Duke Pl.
Dix Hills, NY 11746
---399
John Fragollini
145 TuZZLane
Tanis Boro, jl;AK
LUFTPOST
PAR AVION
PRIORITAIRE
LÉGIPOSTA
PAR AVION
Igor Stravinsky
Old Glory

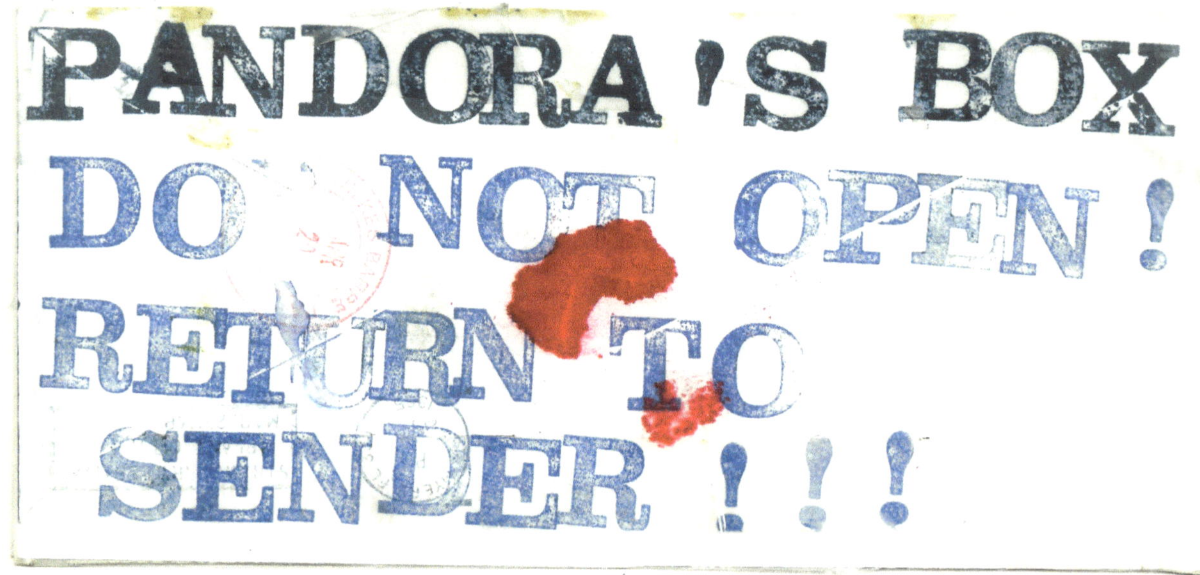
PANDORA'S BOX
DO NOT OPEN!
RETURN TO
SENDER!!!

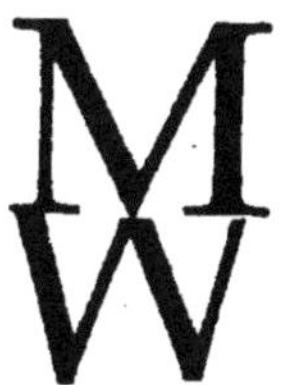

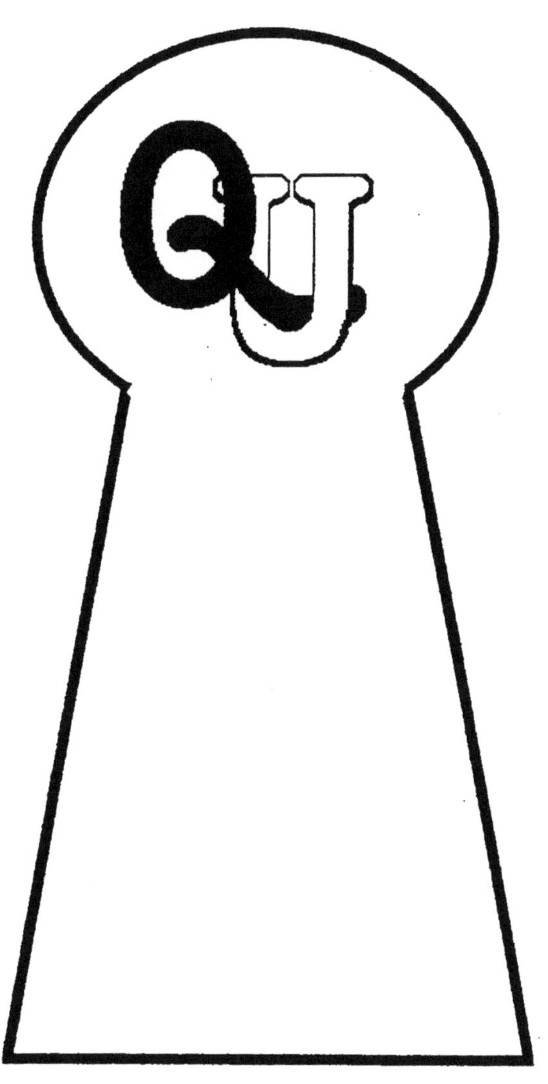

“;;:′.?—(!)-#;;-{?*<~!”

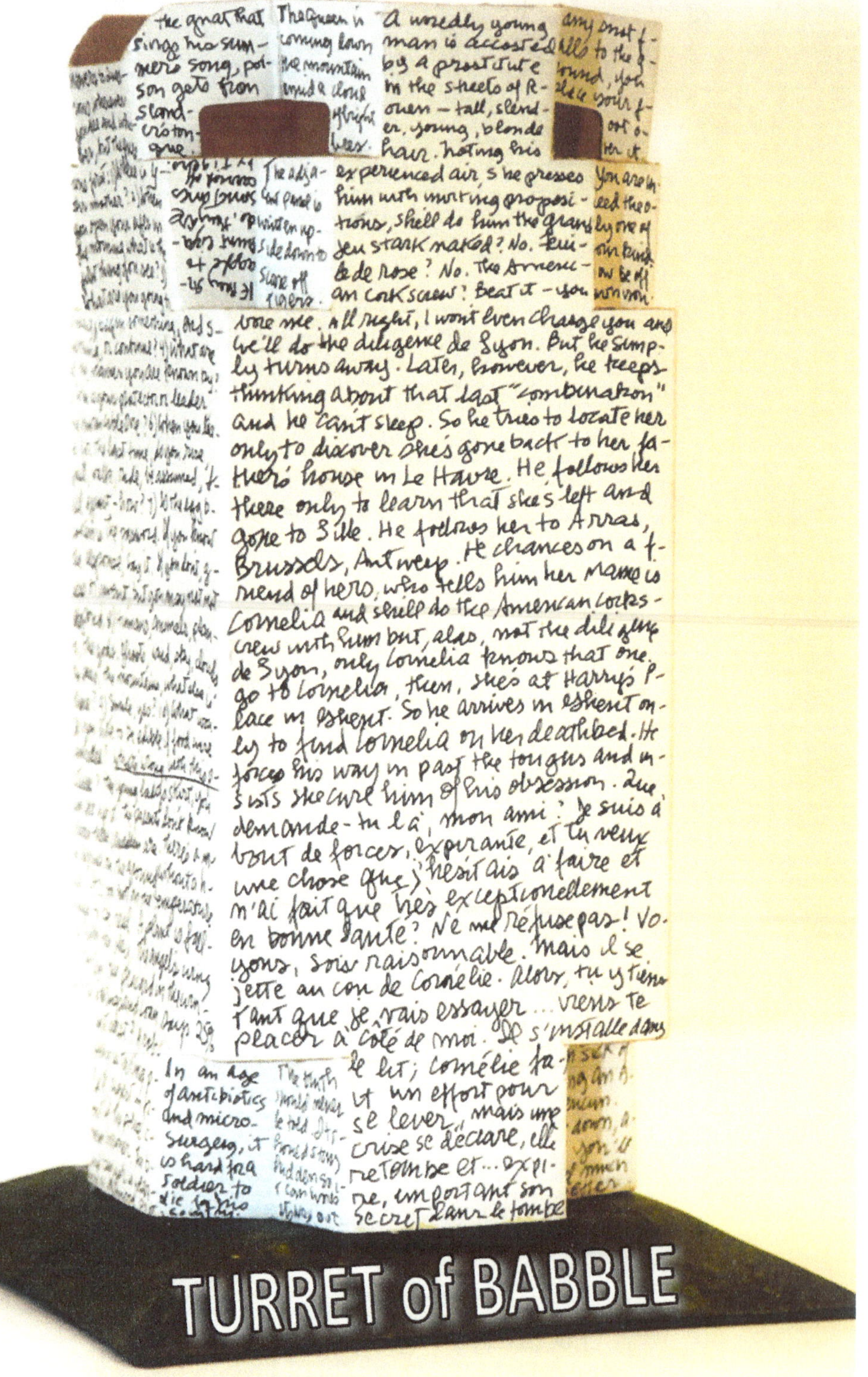

A weedly young man is accosted by a prostitute in the streets of Rouen — tall, slender, young, blonde hair. Noting his experienced air, she presses him with inviting propositions, shell do him the grand jeu stark naked? No. Feuille de rose? No. The American corkscrew? Beat it — you bore me. All right, I wont even charge you and we'll do the diligence de Lyon. But he simply turns away. Later, however, he keeps thinking about that last "combination" and he can't sleep. So he tries to locate her only to discover she's gone back to her father's house in Le Havre. He follows her there only to learn that she's left and gone to Lille. He follows her to Arras, Brussels, Antwerp. He chances on a friend of hers, who tells him her name is Cornelia and she'll do the American corkscrew with him but, alas, not the diligence de Lyon, only Cornelia knows that one. Go to Cornelia, then, she's at Harry's Place in Eshent. So he arrives in Eshent only to find Cornelia on her deathbed. He forces his way in past the tongues and insists she cure him of his obsession. Que demande-tu là, mon ami? Je suis à bout de forces, expirante, et tu veux une chose que j'hésitais à faire et n'ai fait que très exceptionellement en bonne santé? Ne me refuse pas! Voyons, sois raisonnable. Mais il se jette au cou de Cornélie. Alors, tu y tiens tant que je vais essayer... viens te placer à côté de moi. Il s'installe dans le lit; Cornélie fait un effort pour se lever, mais une crise se déclare, elle retombe et... expire, emportant son secret dans la tombe
TURRET of BABBLE

thinking about that last "combination"
and he can't sleep. So he tries to locate her
only to discover she's gone back to her fa-
ther's house in Le Havre. He follows her
there only to learn that she's left and
gone to Lille. He follows her to Arras,
Brussels, Antwerp. He chances on a f-
riend of hers, who tells him her name is
Cornelia and she'll do the American locks-
crew with him but, alas, not the diligence
de Dijon, only Cornelia knows that one.
go to Cornelia, then, she's at Harry's P-
lace in Ghent. So he arrives in Ghent on-
ly to find Cornelia on her deathbed. He
forces his way in past the tongues and in-
sists she cure him of his obsession. She,

Turret Panel Patch Excerpt from La Diligence de Rouen

Once Known As the Dirtiest Joke in the World

it must be true. roses are red. life is all there is. all men a
re mortal. my name is mine own. it is the children who inherit.
yesterday is no more. food is to be eaten. god is good. masters
command, servants obey. if i shut my eyes i cannot see. silence
is deafening. there's more than one penny in the wishing well.
all roads lead to where you are going. the door that was closed
is now open. bones do not get up and walk. tomorrow is anotherd
ay. ancestors haunt. when you reach the end, halt. when you cli
mb the wall, do not let the ladder be removed. learn from your b
etters. the child not a child is an adult. forever is too long.
books are for reading. houses reach to the sky. eventually your
number will be up. trust your doctor. i cannot explain more tha
n i can understand. everyone's cross is hard to bear. lick your
lips to taste the rest. no pencil writes by itself. eggs are me
ant to be broken. at opposite gates stand birth and death. nobo
dy's perfect. unstable as water. if it itches, scratch it. nigh
t is blind. to take one piece is to leave the rest. man is the o
nly animal who knows that he must die. i spent all i have and m
y pockets are bare. mirrors lie. the grass grows greener as the
days improve. try as he will no man can bear a child. bankers a
nd beggars do not mix. the finger points to the guilty party. if
you break my legs i cannot walk. the key that falls to the bott
om of the well avails not him who has fallen beside it. figs do
not grow on thistles nor hairs on a smooth pate. love needs no a
rgument. television is here to stay. dew rusts the naked sword t
hat lies in the open. if you do not laugh the joke is not funny
. when i am weary i go to bed. the lottery rewards only the tic
ket. time will tell. nobody sees behind his back. it is either
penetrate or be penetrated. we meet at the crossroads. until t
he next funeral, then. wait long enough and something is sure t
o happen. boils break as they will. be yourself. nobody knows w
hat you really think. what's yours is yours, what's mine is min
e. burnt fire leaves ash. you only have one mother. try to stop
breathing and you will see what you are up against. says so here, so

unless

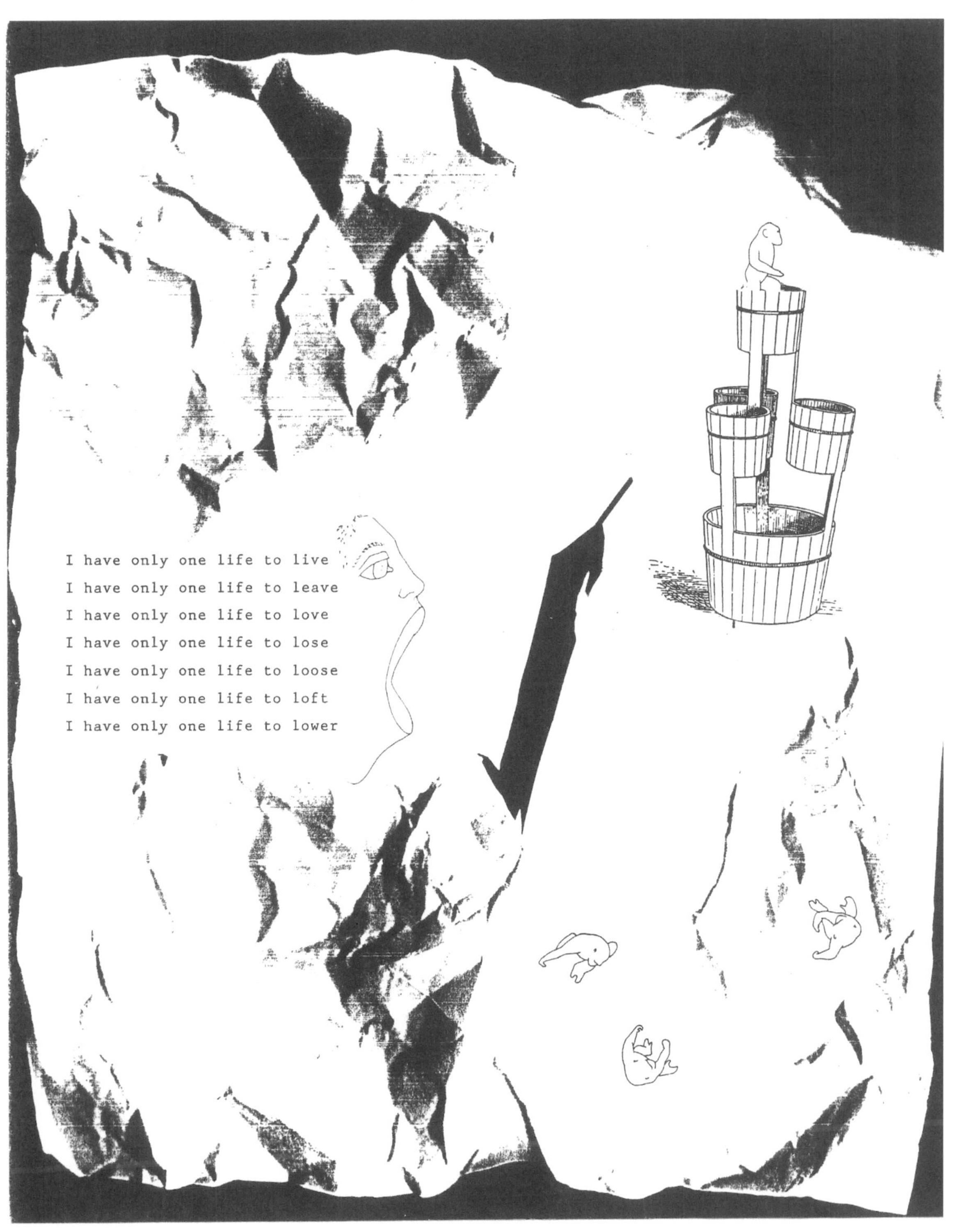
I have only one life to live
I have only one life to leave
I have only one life to love
I have only one life to lose
I have only one life to loose
I have only one life to loft
I have only one life to lower

i.e.

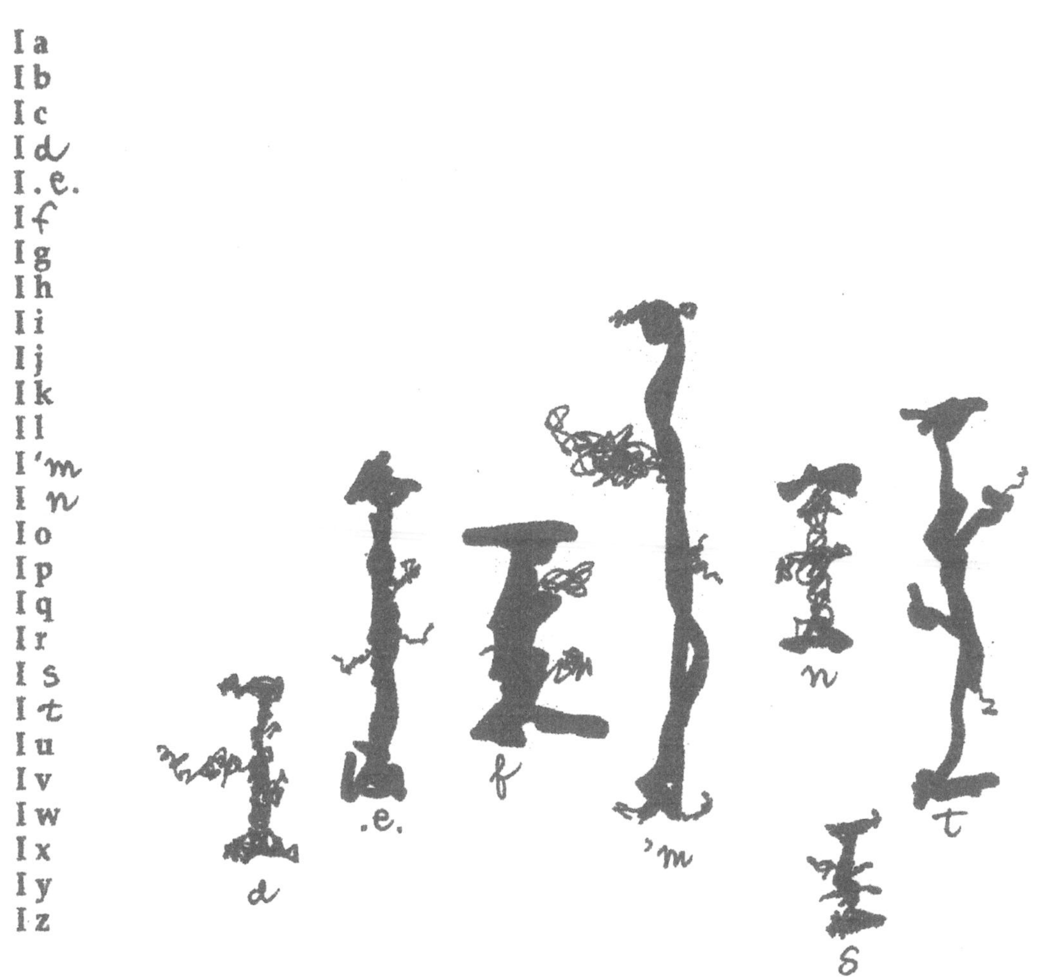

If id is in it, I'm I

Nature and Man Are a Given

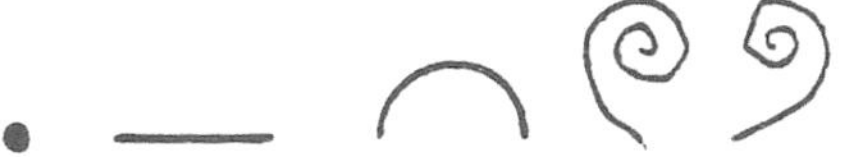

Only Things Have Souls

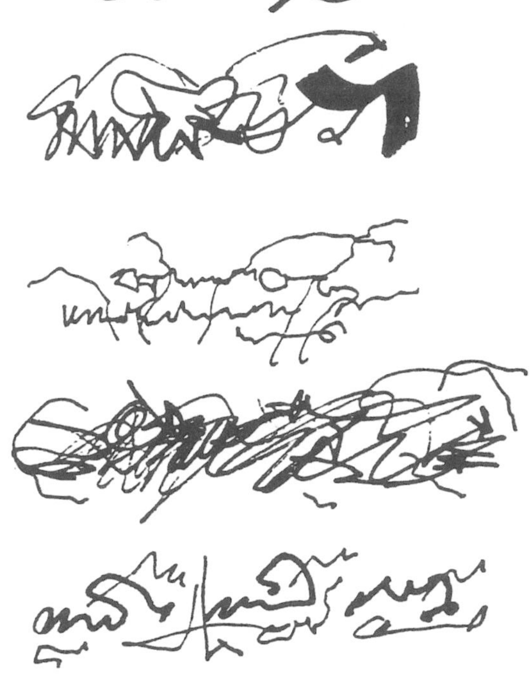

paper clip

steel shaving

plastic bottle cap

forK Lift

light buLb

Of The Contact Between Two Things
Making An Impression One On The Other
Such As Pen Applies
Intelligent Signs Or SymbolsTo Paper
But Often Also Including
Cruder Instruments Depositing
Careless   Accidental   Uncontrollable
Abortive   Rude   Malicious   Baleful   Foul
Indecipherables

IMPACTED

scrawl
overhead leak
sandpapering
defacement, or,
clumsy effacement
slip of the pen
palsied finger smutch
pentimento
botched likeness
palpation skid
dribble splay
seal stamping
crossout
illegible hand
bloodstain
what filthied here?
secret sign
flyspeck
linen fibre decay?
idiot's lovemark
i-dot puncture
inculpating soiling
graffito
erotic symbol
tittle
interrupted smear
slashing wipe
art rubbing
thumbwhorl inktwist
pen trailoff
out out!
penciltwist fill-in
fullstop
exudate

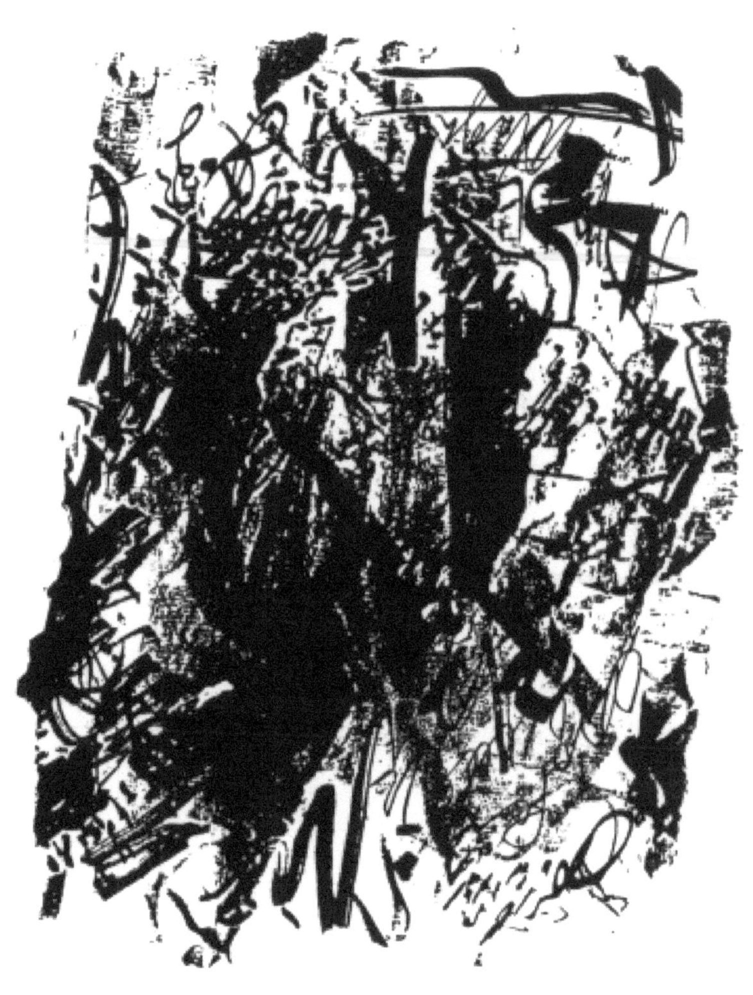

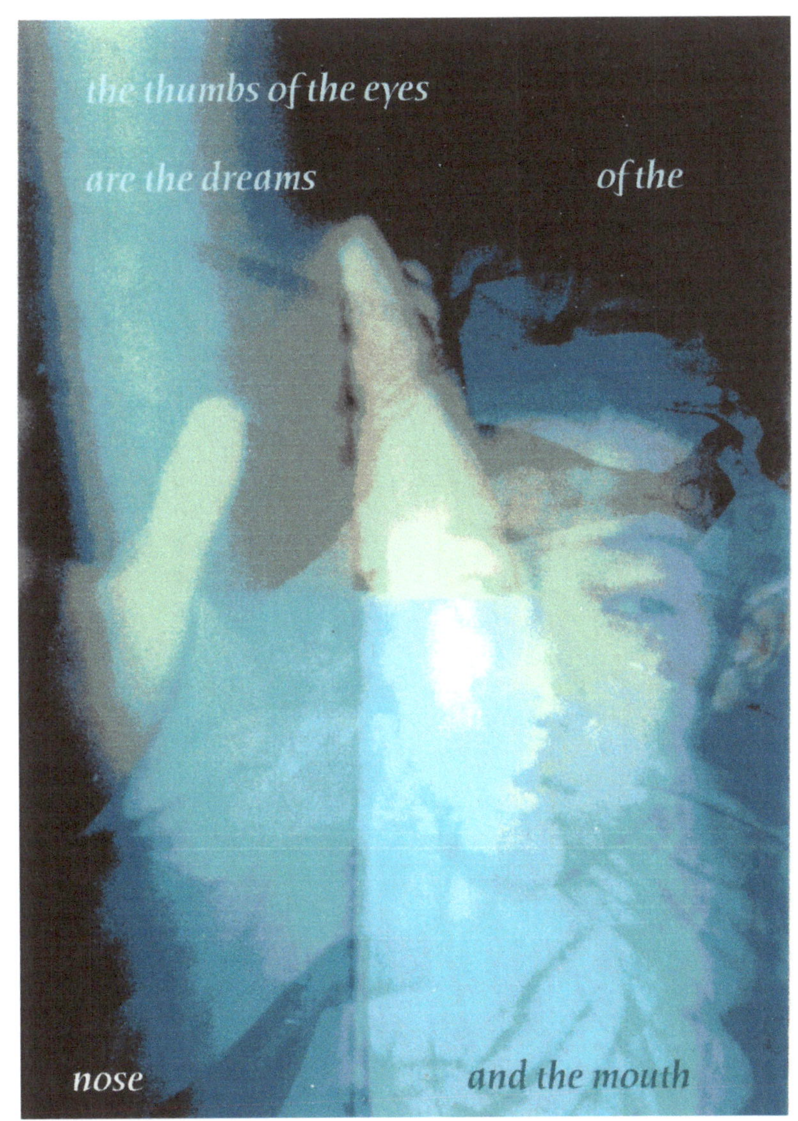
the thumbs of the eyes
are the dreams
of the
nose
and the mouth

Neat Fuss

How do you do
do what I do
be what I do
what can I not now do
be do

Do me I do
I do
Undo me I do
I do
Have you undone me I do
I do
Then am I undone I do
I do
Thy Will Be Done I do make do
Do you see
done with feel
done think
a know
w believe
a
y with I do really mind
I do
I do
I do
I do
Do you take this I do
Do you swear that I do
Dost I do
Thou
Now I do what I do what's to do

Higher Dune or die Dune OK

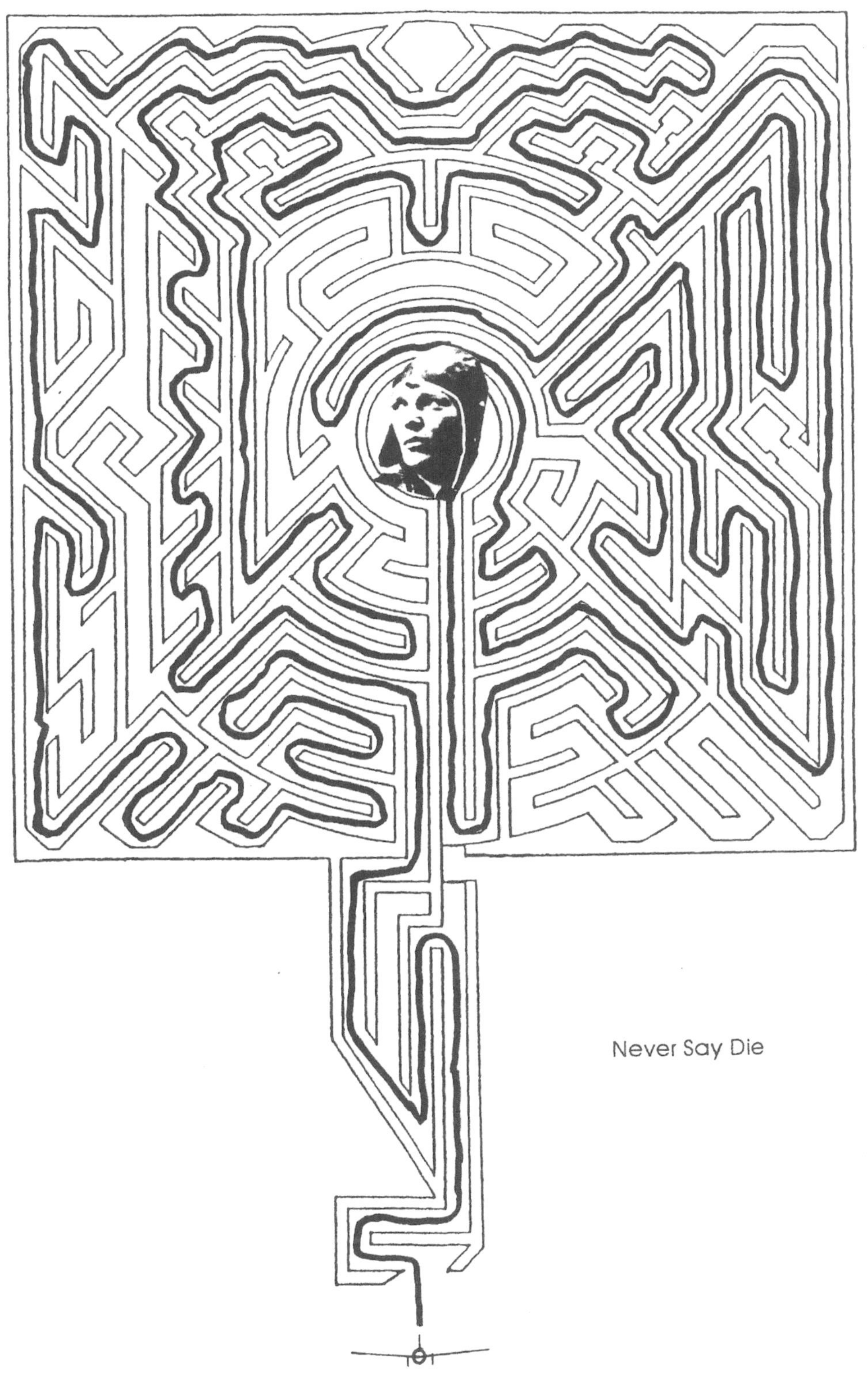

Never Say Die

SIMULATION TEST

COMPLETE THIS PERFORMANCE FORM*

the straight line **found nowhere in nature**

in the sense that

"no woman can throw a ball like a man"

****

draw a straight line freehand below like an "artist":

draw a straight line freehand below like anyone else:

draw a line deliberately crooked below the way an "artist" would draw it:

draw a deliberately crooked line below knowing perfectly well you couldn't draw a straight line freehand anyway:

---

*If you are an "artist" simulate not being one.

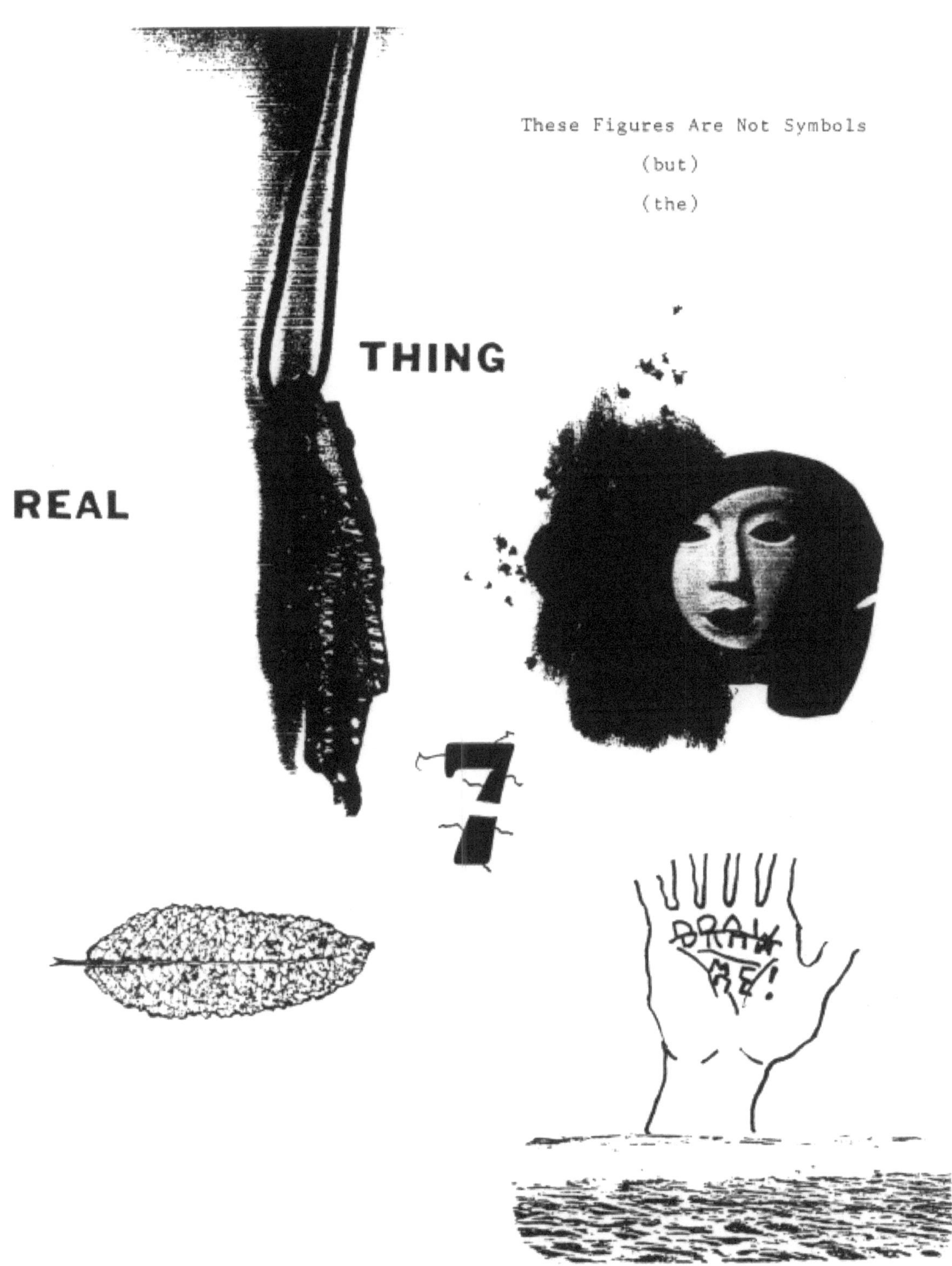
These Figures Are Not Symbols
(but)
(the)
THING
REAL
7
DRAW
ME!

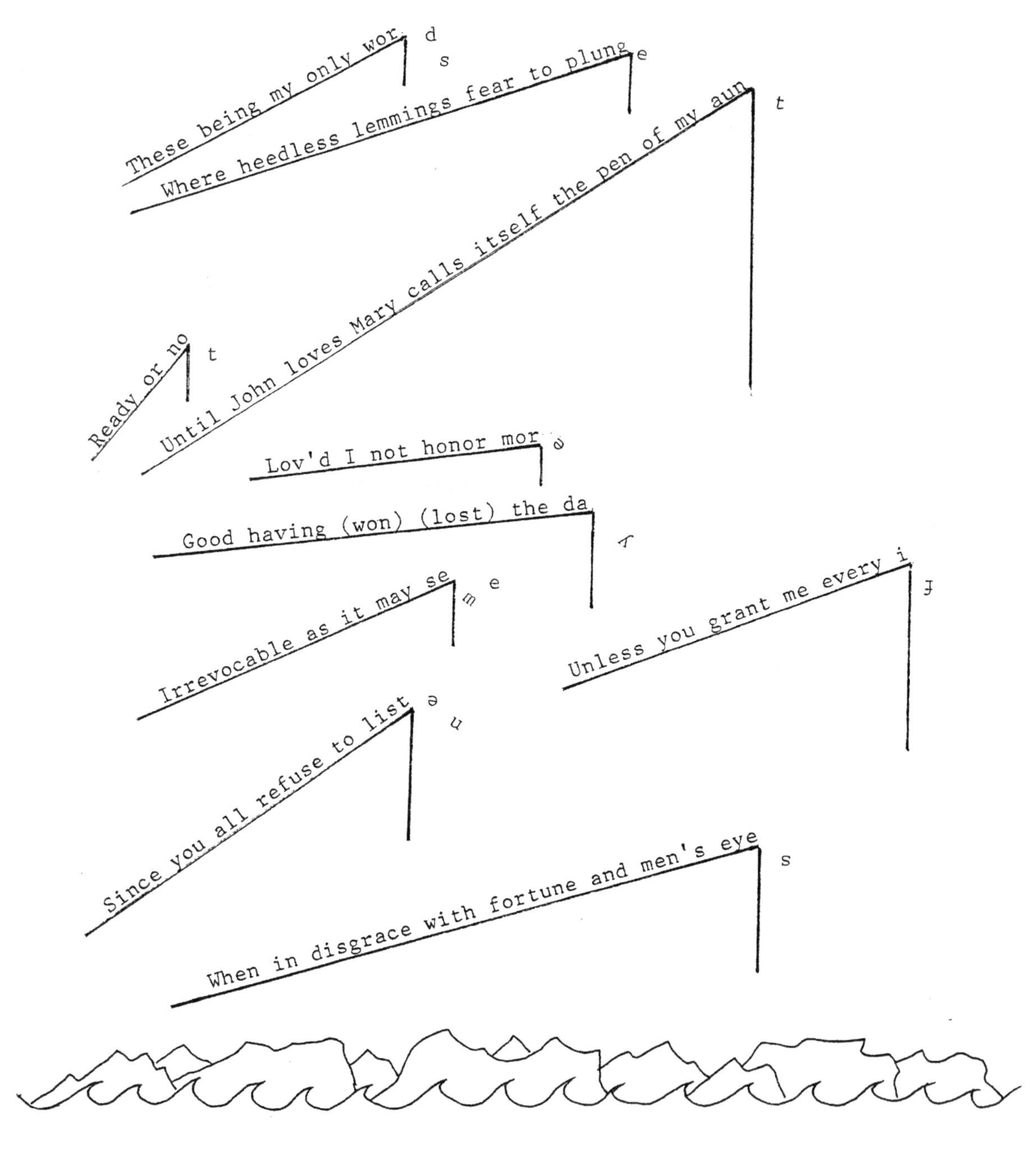
These being my only words
Where heedless lemmings fear to plunge
Until John loves Mary calls itself the pen of my aunt
Ready or not
Lov'd I not honor more
Good having (won) (lost) the dark
Irrevocable as it may seem
Unless you grant me every if
Since you all refuse to listen
When in disgrace with fortune and men's eyes

Seventeen Vertical Long Thin Metal Tubes. Sufficiently alike in appearance as to present a Minimal version of imitative complicity. Sufficiently different in alloys admixed, reflection of light along surface hues, and deceptive impression of weight as to look separately identifiable. The concave wall of each tube is engraved a few centimetres from the top with the alchemical sign of its principal mineral base, as those for copper, lead, tin, iron, etc.

These indications do not appear in the diagram above.

However, if an imaginary line is diagonally run from uppermost left to lowermost right, it will be seen that five of the tubes are physically interrupted as if a small piece had been removed from each, as in the diagram: their signifying marks are assigned, as shown in the right margin of this accounting, as left to right in the diagram respectively corresponding to top to bottom in the figures in the margin. Nevertheless, the integrity of each such tube is questionable; whether or not the interruption in length creates two tubes or is to be understood merely as an unoccupied part of the whole, whether we have here two separate pieces uneasily brought together under the same identification or single wholes despite appearances.

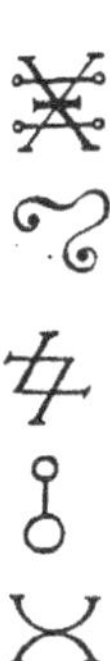

The diagram and this accounting are all that is known about the real thing Seventeen Vertical Long Thin Metal Tubes and may therefore be construed together as representing it: a composite word-and-image Found Object, discovered several years ago—the accounting crumpled into a ball and stuffed inside one of the tubes—by an artist known only as The Finder and now in the collection of the __________Foundation. The Tubes have never been exhibited or photographed, so that their reality and validity are for all ascertainable purposes indistinguishable from their reputation here attested.

Actually there are only fifteen long thin vertical metal tubes (count them), no matter the seventeen assumed by the verbal rendering. This discrepancy is at best only discussible since it is part of the entire work.

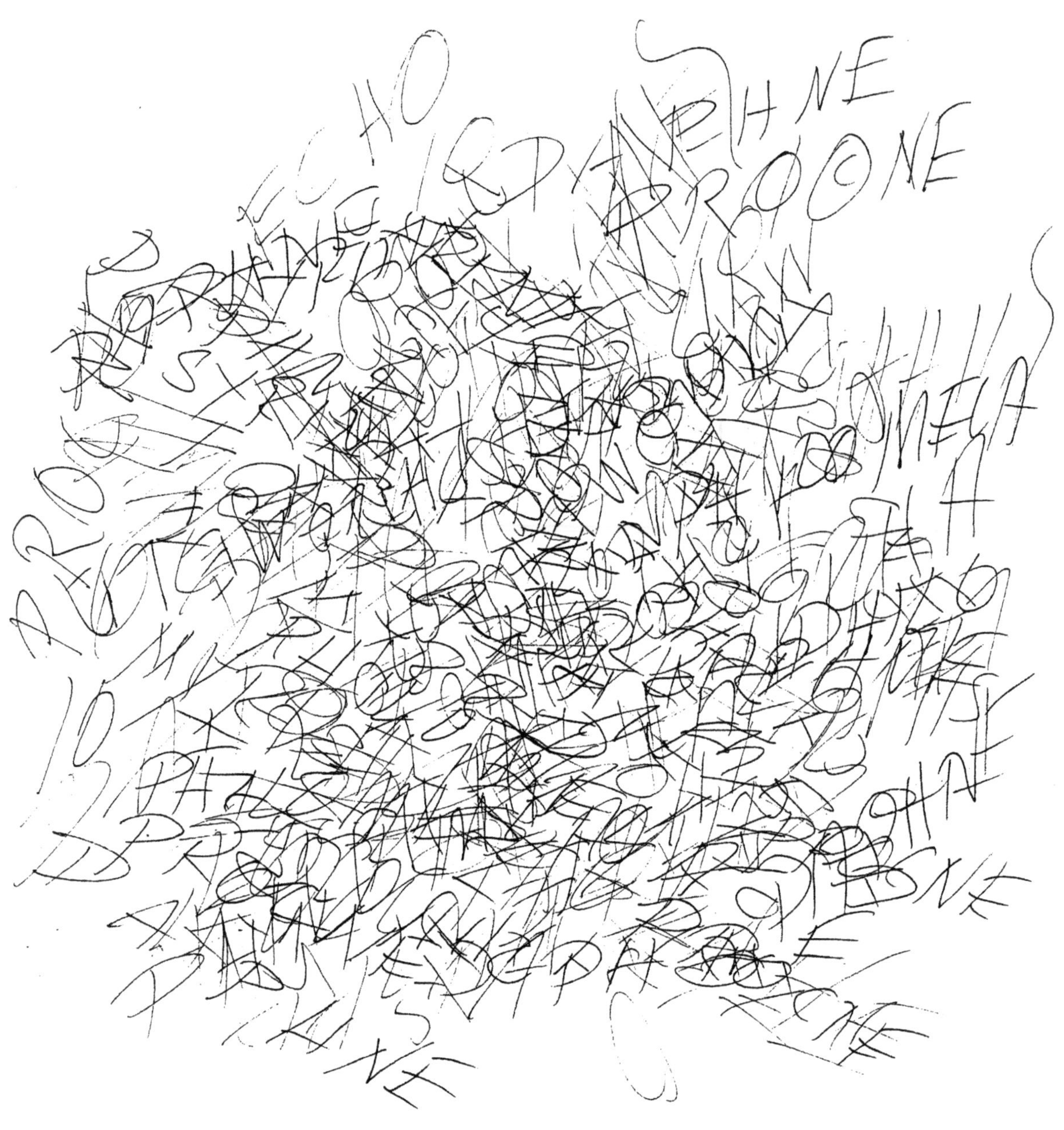

She Was Here a Moment Ago

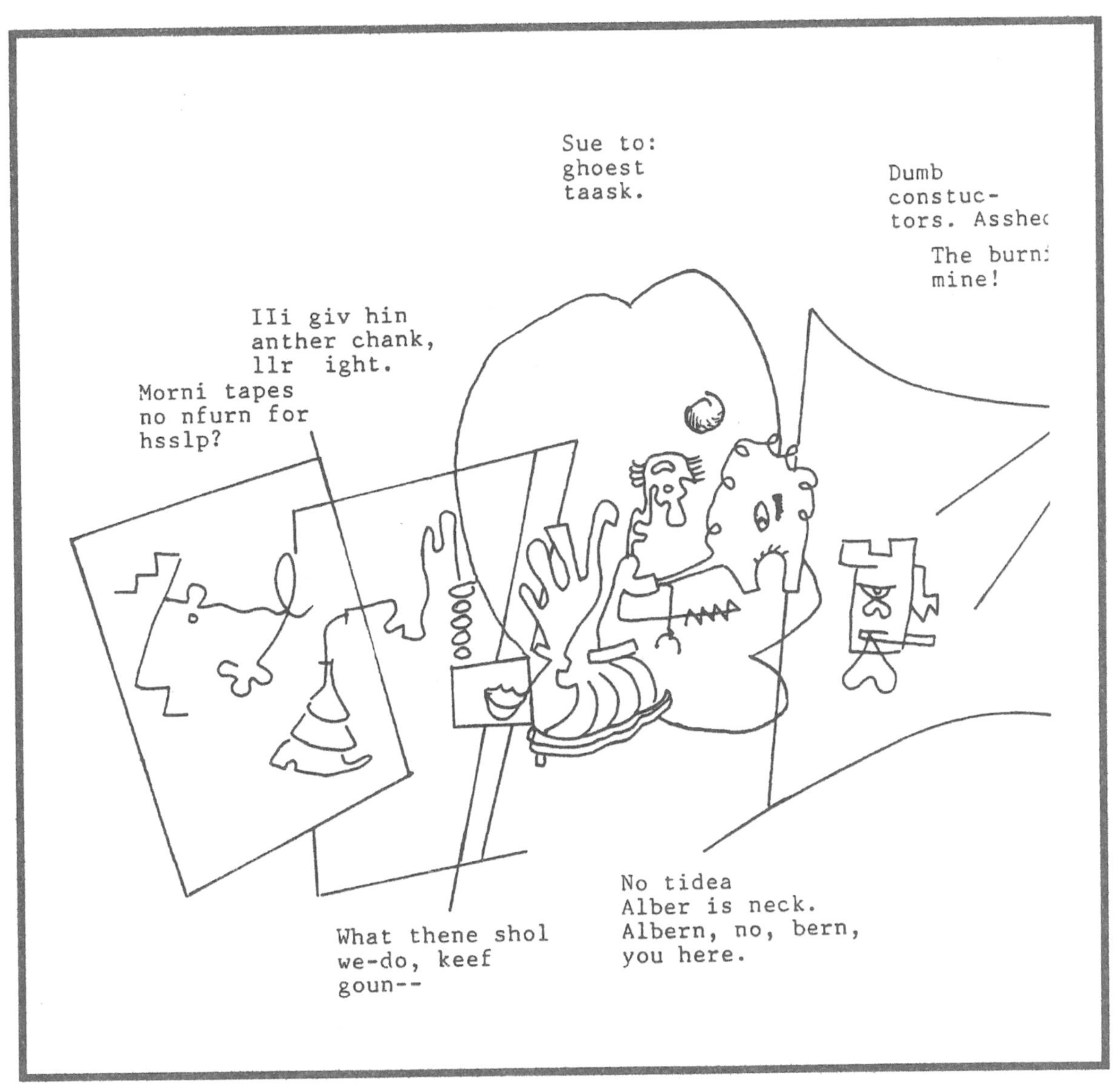

SITCOM ANDERGINNIES

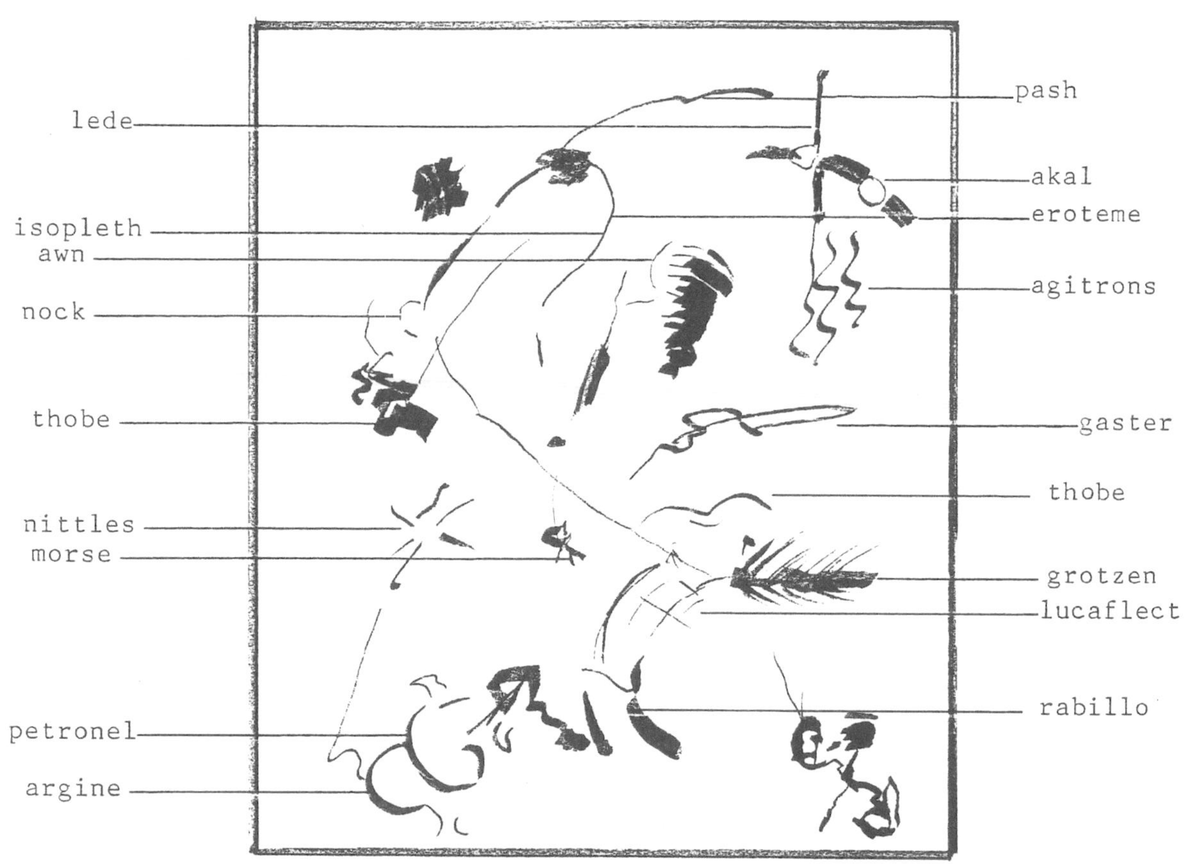

Untitled, 1992, ink on paper, 11X13cm

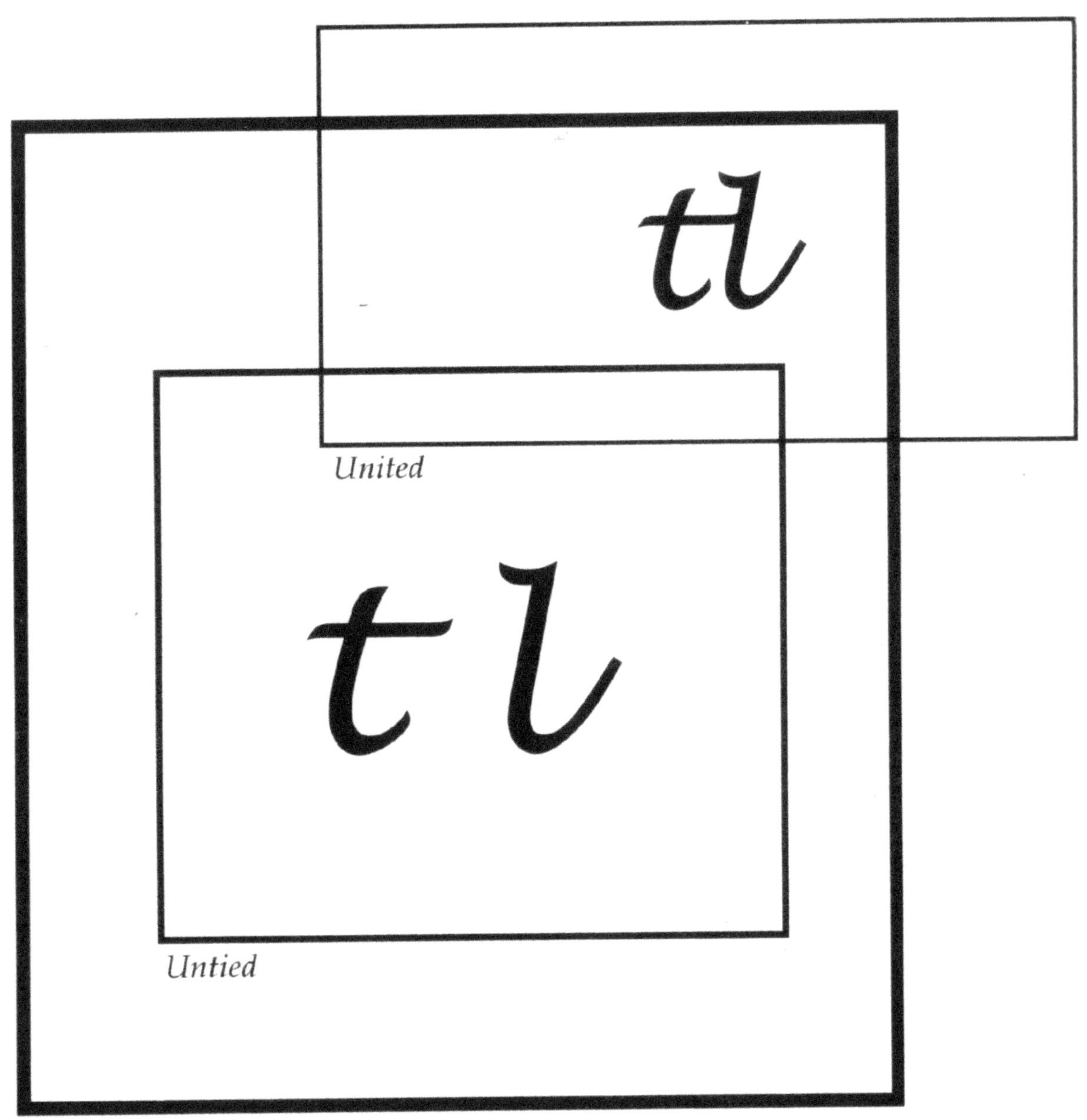

Untitled

TET

PAPATATAP

PEPET put-put poptop tiptop tut-tut TEP

PIPITITIP

POPOTOTOP

PUPUTUTUP

these lines
have things coming out of them
squirming in different directions

the things
coming out of these lines
protrude or shoot

while lines like these
simply stand their ground
their things "prolapsed"

unless you force them out yourself
nobody looking
your poem

Tracking

Sandy, full of gorse
Give them suckle
Incredible hilarity
I sing to animals
The bliss of torment
Buzz off, you guys
To void the obvious
What Plato really meant

— Z O N E S —

Doves	embrace	in the skies	of the spiritual	father	Upper
Dogs	engage	on the earth	of the selfish	child	Middle
Eels	hump	in the seas	of the sensual	mother	Lower

— D I R E C T I O N —

dark shadows ⟷ the young and the restless

— P R E S S U R E —

PASTY & POWERFUL faint & fugitive

— SLANT —

dignity

defiance compliance

supine collapse — prone exhaustion

— RHYTHM —

heartbeat

chatter

chainsaw

TO ΧΑΟΣ

+-+-+-+-COSMIC JUSTICE+-+-+-+-

(G—D)

mananima

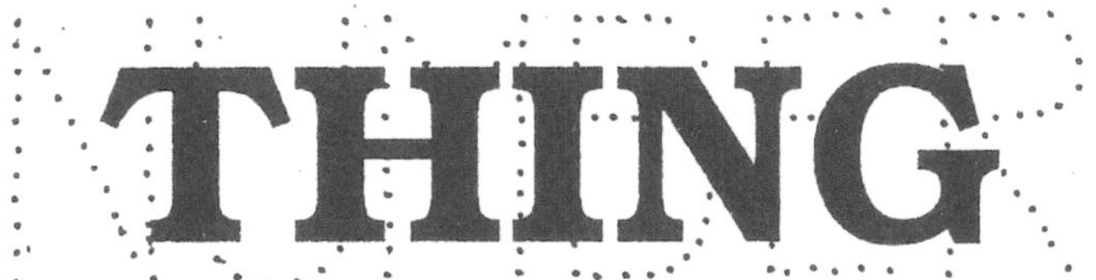

art   artifact   trash/other matter
invisibly
contingent on purpose and place
wherever it belongs
gravity-bound or in orbit

includes hallucinations
and surrealist/postmodern
evasions and collusions

the ring on the finger
the airplane in the sky

excludes windborne shreds
of cotton wool
torn newsprint
ripped plastic

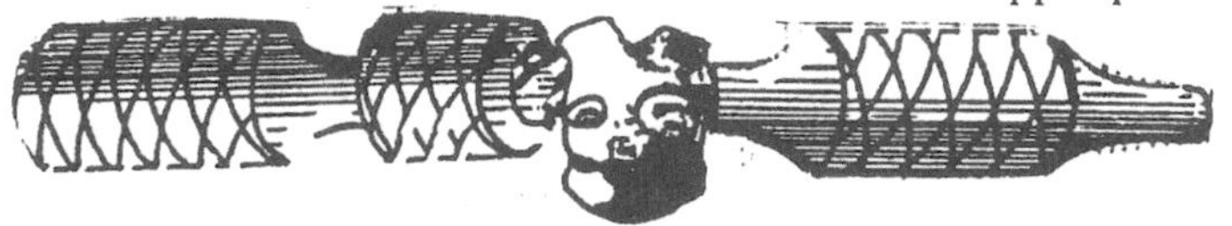

THING-AS-THING MADE **VISIBLE**
THROWS THE WORLD OUT OF KILTER
INFLUENCE ON MAN'S FATE UNDETERMINED

SKEWED FIT
lost and missed:
cuff link under the refrigerator
lost? and found by another:
whose is that gasket in the
flower bed?
suddenly come upon:
what is this brick kiln doing here?

NAMELESSNESS
fragment/broken off section
forlorn inventions
Rome: 19th-century cowpasture
with marble objects protruding

UTTER BEWILDERMENT
the paper clip in the sand dune
the stone ax on the carpet

WHAT'S WRONG WITH THIS PICTURE ?

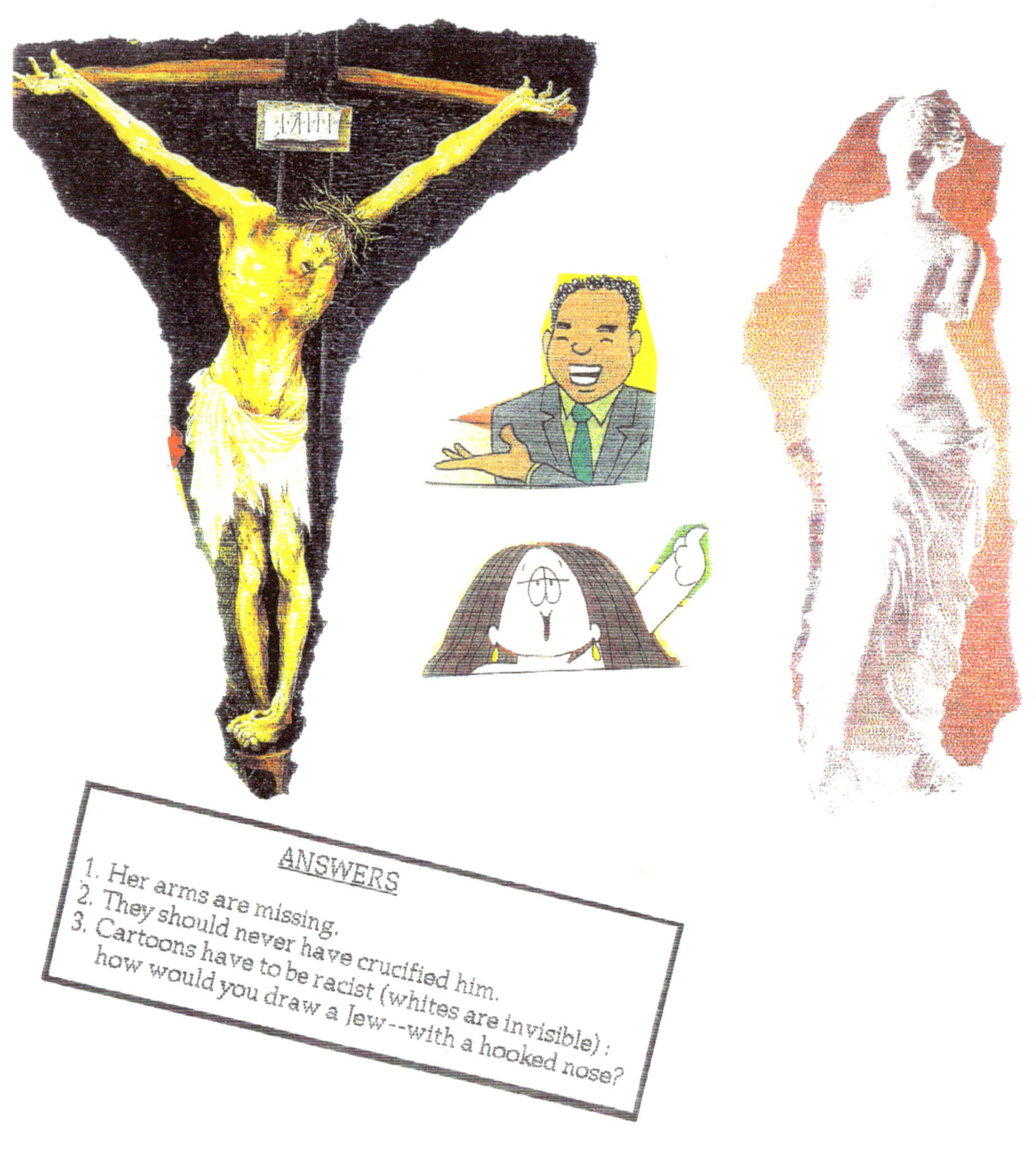

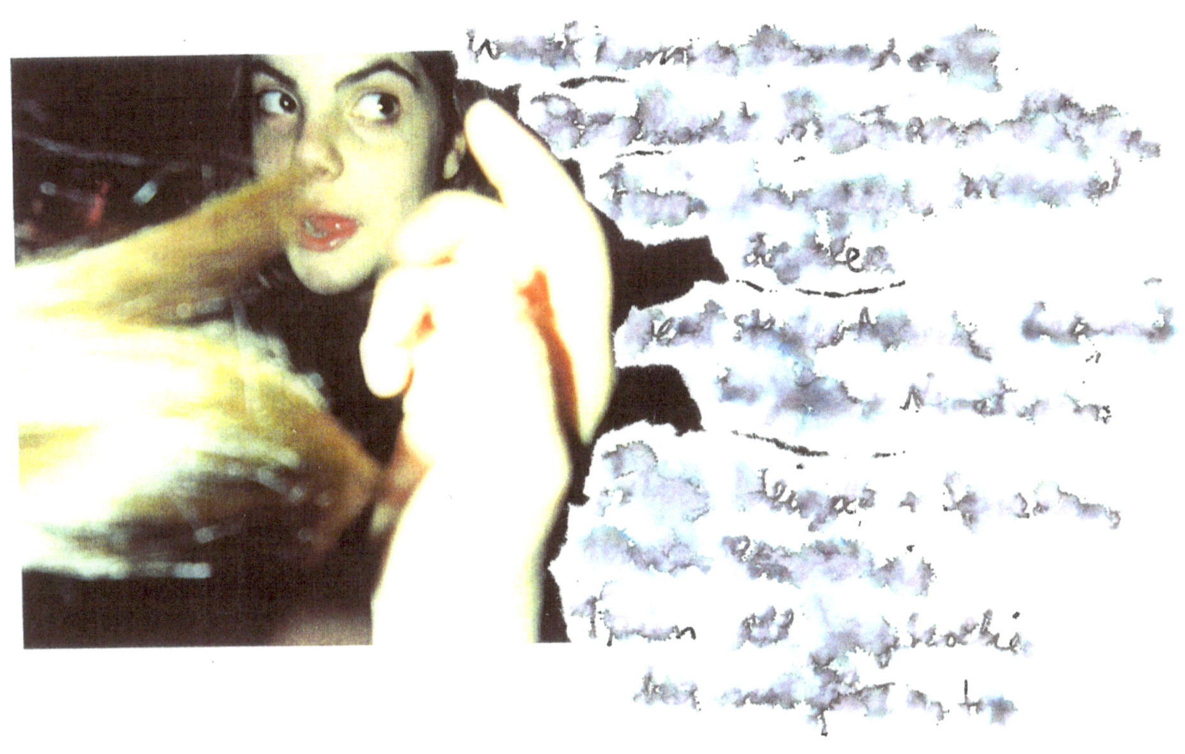

ωηατ τηε σιρεν σανγ

Life Is Violent: **TO BRAYE**

The General Kinds of Violent Motion may be known as:

Translation
into a new place

Dissolution of Union
in the same Body

Some impression
from the Mover, as in:

Striking	Knocking	Pecking	Pounding
Percussion	beating	Mattock	contusion
swinge	Blow	Pick-Ax	stamp
smite	butt		**BRAY-ING**
bang	mallet		
beat	battering		
bast	jobbing		
buffet	ramm		
cuff			
dash			
hit			
swinge			
thump			
blow			
strike			
slap			
rap			
tap			
flap			
kick			
wince			
spurn			
bob			
box			
fillip			
whirret			
skit			
pummel			
punch			
rebuff			
yerke			
collide			
gnash			
repercussion			
interfere			
let fly at			

(uniteputcloseconjoinmakenear)

The Sundry Kinds of Operations are such Laborious
Pains or Play, as:

THOUGH THOU SHOULDEST **BRAYE**
[brek-an, brayen: beat smal
l or bruise, pound, crush t
o powder, crush with a brak
e, temper & spread, scour,t
hrash, beat in a morter, br
ay the brawn of, bray the b
lood from, bray betwixt]A F
OOL WITH A PESTELL IN A MOR
TER LIKE OTEMEEELE, YET WIL
L HIS FOOLISHENESSE NOT GOE
FROM HIM. Coverdale, Prov.
xxvii, 22.

Travail
Toil
moile
Turmoile
drudge
work
handy-work
Ply
co-operate
take pains
lay about him
spurt
spirt
Sport
lusory
dally, in:

Ordinary & Mixed Mechanical Operations performed by:

(formshapehammeroutfashion)

Lever
Balance
Wedge
Pulley
Wheel
Screw Spring
Crank
Winch

Agriculture, Sartorian, Chymical & Fabrile Operations of:

Dissolution of Continuity by:

Division or Separation in:

Shaving or Contusion

bruising
pounding
stamping
morter
pestell
BRAY-ING

REAKSSCISSORS
WHATDIDID
CUTPAPERCOVER
OTODESER
SSTONEBREAKSS
VETHISHA
CISSORSCUTPAPE
PPENTOME
RCOVERSSTONEB

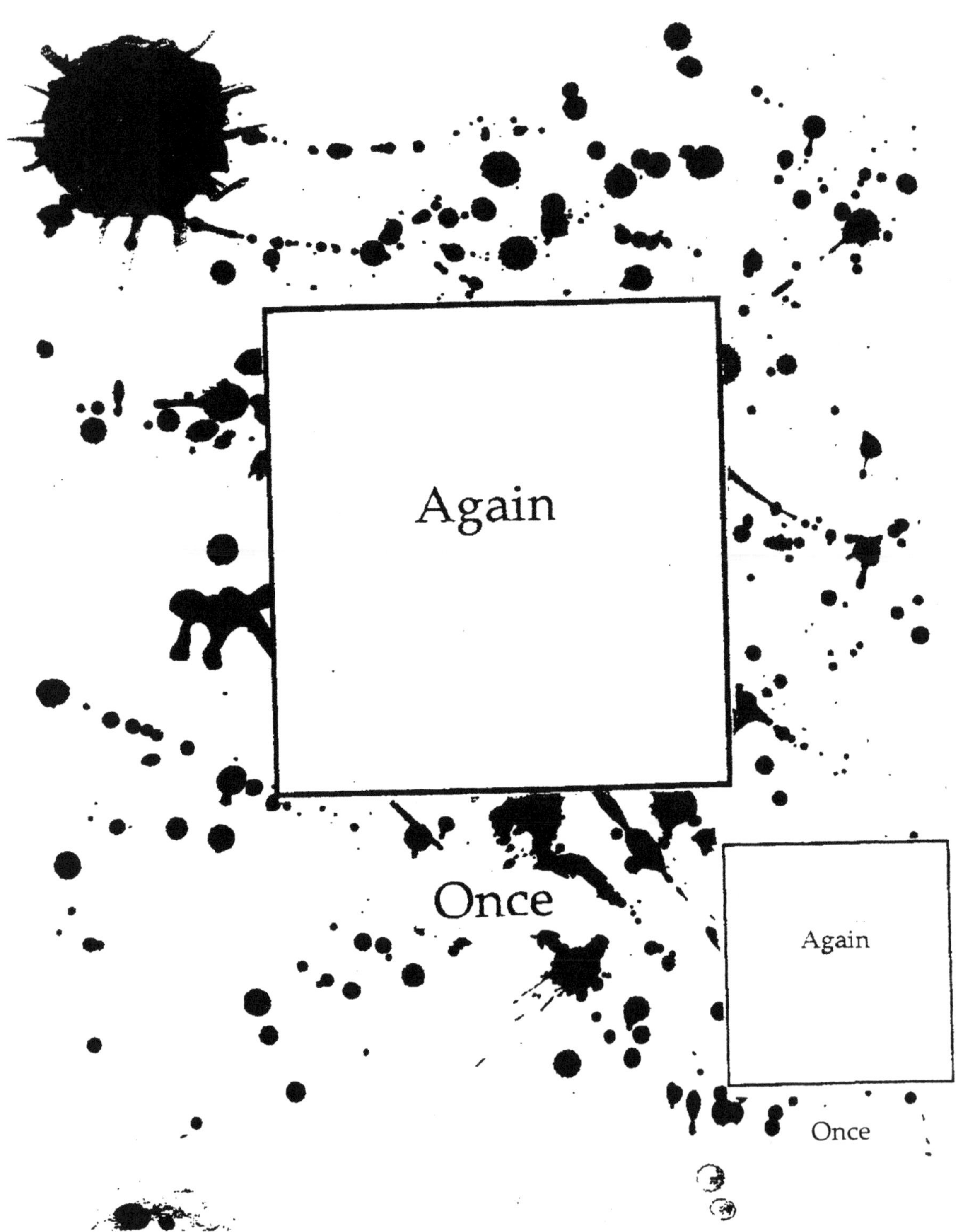
Again
Once
Again
Once

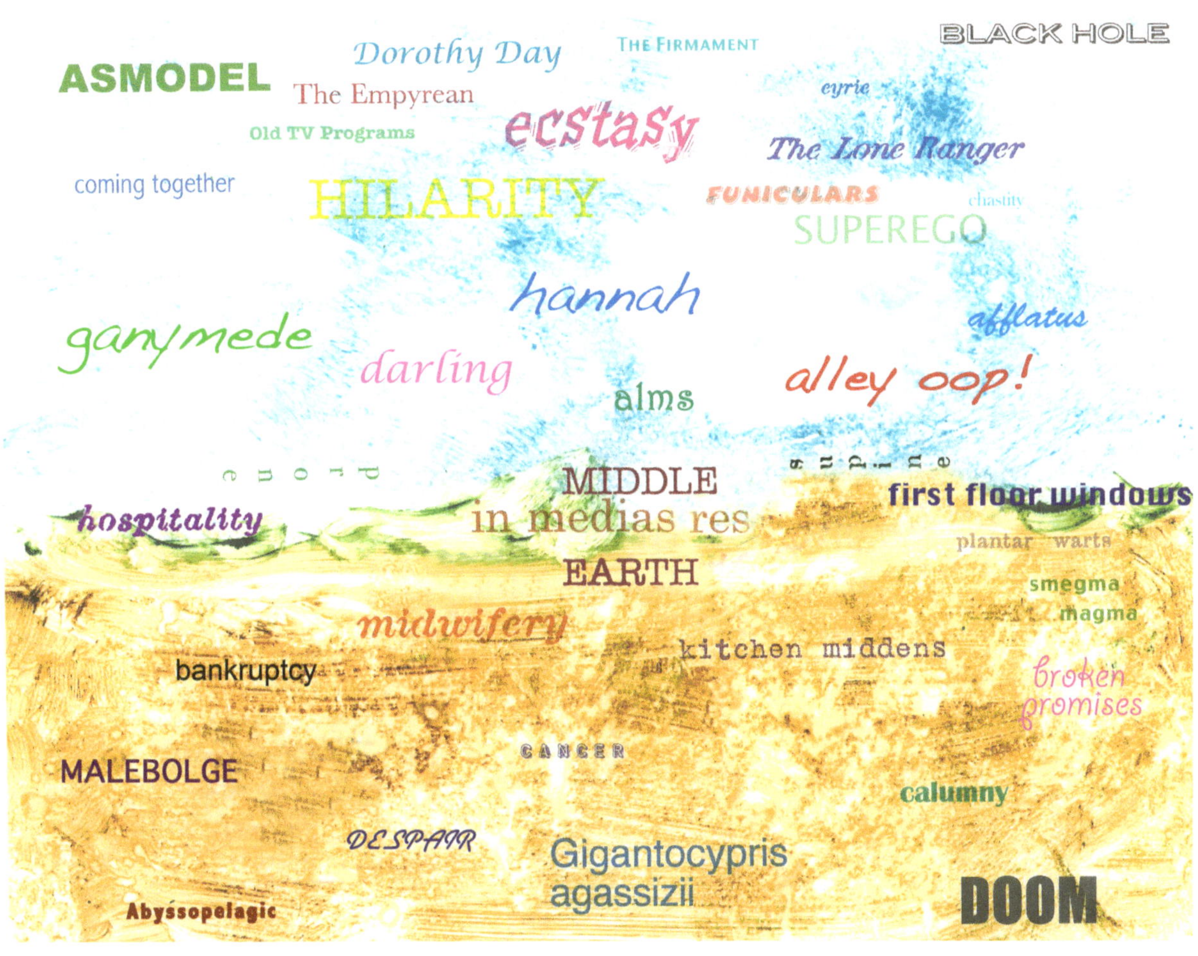

BLACK HOLE
Dorothy Day
THE FIRMAMENT
ASMODEL
The Empyrean
eyrie
Old TV Programs
ecstasy
The Lone Ranger
coming together
HILARITY
FUNICULARS
chastity
SUPEREGO
hannah
afflatus
ganymede
darling
alley oop!
alms
prone
supine
MIDDLE
first floor windows
hospitality
in medias res
plantar warts
EARTH
smegma
magma
midwifery
kitchen middens
bankruptcy
broken promises
CANCER
MALEBOLGE
calumny
DESPAIR
Gigantocypris agassizii
DOOM
Abyssopelagic

The Poet Stands Behind His Name

IrvingIrvingIrvingIrvingIrvingIrvingIrving
IrvingIrvingIrvingIrvingIrvingIrvingIrving
IrvingIrvingIrvingIrvingIrvingIrvingIrving
IrvingIrvingIrvingIrvingIrvingIrvingIrving
IrvingIrvingIrvingIrvingIrvingIrvingIrving
IrvingIrvingIrvingIrvingIrvingIrvingIrving
IrvingIrvingIrvingIrvingIrvingIrvingIrving
IrvingIrvingIrvingIrvingIrvingIrvingIrving
IrvingIrvingIrvingIrvingIrvingIrvingIrving
IrvingIrvingIrvingIrvingIrvingIrvingIrving
IrvingIrvingIrvingIrvingIrvingIrvingIrving
IrvingIrvingIrvingIrvingIrvingIrvingIrving
IrvingIrvingIrvingIrvingIrvingIrvingIrving
IrvingIrvingIrvingIrvingIrvingIrvingIrving
IrvingIrvingIrvingIrvingIrvingIrvingIrving
IrvingIrvingIrvingIrvingIrvingIrvingIrving

Identities by Irving Weiss
Printed in the Autonomous Republic of Qazingulaza

www.ingramcontent.com/pod-product-compliance
Lightning Source LLC
LaVergne TN
LVHW070137110826
845147LV00002B/270

* 9 7 8 1 9 3 6 6 8 7 0 4 6 *